MW01199773

THE FORK IN THE ROAD

My Personal Faith Journey

Also written by Cindy Mallin:

Simple Trust, Simple Prayers:
Life-Changing Lessons from the Journals of George
Mueller

Co-written with Mickey Mallin
Simply Trusting God:
Living the Lessons of George Mueller In the 21st
Century

The Fork in the Road

My Personal Faith Journey

Cindy Mallin

Yellow Bus Publishing

The Fork in the Road by Cindy Mallin
Published by Yellow Bus Publishing
The Villages, Florida 32163

Requests for information should be addressed to:
CindyMallin@gmail.com
MickeyMallin@gmail.com

ISBN: 9781672812337

Printed in the United States of America

This book is dedicated to one person. I do not know this person's name yet, but I hope to soon.

If you make a decision to follow Jesus as a result of reading this book, then YOU are the person.

This book is dedicated to you.

Contents

CHAPTER 1

"Wait – you were a Christian through all that mess and you never gave up?"

That was Mickey's biggest question for me back in 2005 when we first met. We spent time telling each other our stories. Where did we come from? How did we get here?

As I told the short version of my own story, Mickey heard how central my faith journey was to all my 50+ years of life. To his non-Christian (Jewish) ears, there was something that didn't make sense to him.

So that was his question. "Why didn't you walk away from your faith?"

Especially as he learned that my first marriage was a 22-year marriage to… a minister. It didn't make sense to him that I would still be holding on to faith – stronger than ever.

Back then, I gave him a short version, something like this:

"Are you kidding? I would NEVER walk away from God! Never, never, NEVER! My faith was the single thing that kept me going all those years!"

The longer version? Well, that's what is now written in the pages that follow. As I remember the memories and feel the feelings again, I have often wept … again.

Yeah, me… the basic person-who-doesn't-cry. Me. Brought to tears again.

But though it may be true that much of my history has been hard, and often sad, through it all I see the fingerprints of God's own hand.

And that's what I want everyone to see!

I don't want this to be another sad story about someone's life. I want it to be my true story, and when I look back at it all, I now see God's fingerprints everywhere!

Yes, I will describe some days and events that sound pretty sad. And wrong even. But it's my story, and it's all true.

As I've gotten older, I also realized that my own kids and other extended family members don't know the journey my own faith has taken me. It seems like it's time to write this down.

Each person's story is different and unique. This is my story.

CHAPTER 2

"Come and hear, all you who fear God; let me tell you what he has done for me" (Psalm 66:16).

I was born in 1949, the third of six children, all born within a nine-year span of time. The first three were girls, born about a year and a half apart. Then there was a 4-year span with no more children, followed by three more in rapid succession (one year apart). So there were two distinct groups of kids: the "Older Girls" and the "Babes." That's how we were known.

The Older Girls. That's me on the left.

The Older Girls. I am on the left.

As you can tell from these pictures, we weren't even close to what anyone would call affluent. We were poor. Raised in the country in the hills of Pennsylvania by a dad who didn't even finish high school and a mom who had her hands full raising six kids born in nine years.

We wore hand-me-downs, and we ate what Mom put on the table, or we'd go hungry. We wore what we had and we knew better than to complain.

For some reason, I really love these pictures. Maybe because it reminds me where I come from. It reminds me that being poor is not an obstacle for God. He still wanted me. He had a plan for me. Just thinking about that today still amazes me.

Here is the house we grew up in.

At some point, the six of us were sent to Sunday School every Sunday morning. Mom didn't even have a driver's license, so Dad would drive us to a little country church, drop us off, and pick us up an hour later. It must have been Mom's idea because she seemed to have some awareness of Christianity. It certainly would not have come from Dad, a total atheist as far as we knew.

It also gave Mom an hour or two without kids running around.

Sunday mornings while the six kids were gone, Mom would listen to the local radio station to hear a local preacher preach a sermon. As we grew older, we realized she seemed to know some hymns, but maybe she learned those from the Sunday morning radio program.

Mom's parents were active participants in their local "spiritualist" church, and in fact, Mom and Dad were married in a spiritualist "church." (Spiritualist churches are not really churches at all. The movement began in the late 1800s, and was known for séances, "spirit guides," and mediums.)

> *See God's fingerprints? He protected me from the spiritualist movement.*

So our Sunday morning routine was getting our Sunday clothes on (choosing one of the two or three good dresses we had) and all six kids piling into the family station wagon for Dad to drive us to a little country church. Initially, it was a Nazarene church in Bradford, but something happened (we don't know what), and we switched to an Evangelical United Brethren (EUB) church in Lewis Run (which eventually merged into the United Methodist Church).

Divided into classes, we were taught Bible stories by women who meant well and did their best to cover the assigned curriculum.

> *See God's fingerprints? As young children, we went to Sunday School where we learned Bible stories.*

During our early childhood years, my two older sisters and I became known throughout our small town as "The Walb Girls." We sang songs in three-part harmony.

Mom taught us. Every evening after dinner, we Older Girls had to help clean up the kitchen. Mom always washed the dishes, rinsed them, and stacked them in a rack for us to dry. Two of us dried the dishes and one of us swept the kitchen floor. Each week, assignments rotated (important to keep peace).

And one other thing Mom did to maintain peace. She taught us to sing. We didn't talk. We didn't argue. We sang our way through the kitchen chores. Once we learned a basic tune, she would teach one sister the middle part, and another sister the lower part. She did it all from memory.

This actually began when we were pretty young. Recently, I asked my sisters how old we were when we began singing in public. They confirmed my own memories. I was about five or six; they were seven or eight.

As the youngest of the three, I was assigned the lead part, which I really didn't like at all. The introvert in me did not want people listening primarily to my voice. And I did not have a high voice at all, and the lead part usually included some pretty high notes.

We sang in churches, including our own little country church. I have a distinct memory from what must have been my very first time to sit through a church service. Prior to that, we just went to Sunday School.

But on this day, we were scheduled to sing a song – a hymn that Mom had taught us in three-part harmony.

So on that Sunday, the three of us Older Girls were sitting in the pews (neither Mom or Dad ever came) when suddenly I saw something I'd never seen before. Some men dressed in suits were passing a fancy wooden "plate" down each row. When it came to our row, I couldn't believe what I saw: there was money in the plate!

I thought that was awesome, and I reached my hand in to take just a dollar. Not much. I didn't want to be greedy. I just picked up a dollar.

Thankfully, somebody intervened; I don't remember who it was. How was I supposed to know? There was no one to teach me. I put it back.

Did you know redheads blush really easily? Especially introverts.

I had a lot to learn…

And then there was the time we Older Girls were invited to sing one of our three-part harmony hymns in one of the other small churches in town.

We had never been in this church before, but that didn't matter. We went where we were invited. Neither Mom nor Dad ever came in to see us. Dad never stepped foot in a church, and Mom had to tend to the Babes.

The church pianist was going to accompany us, and we were supposed to sing all four verses of the hymn. We only knew the words to the first verse, so we had a hymnal to read the words to the other three verses.

Except... the sister who was supposed to bring the hymnal to the front... didn't. I don't even know which of us was supposed to have it. But the pianist didn't notice, and she just kept playing the hymn... four times. We only knew the first verse.

We were just kids! What did we do? We stood there embarrassed as can be, looking at each other and mumbling something through until finally, mercifully, it ended and we could return to our seats.

That is one memory I would like to forget. It is pretty funny when I look back on it, but then? It was embarrassing.

Somehow, in our little country church, I did manage to learn the basics of the gospel. And then there was that experience from summer camp.

There must have been a scholarship fund that paid our way. So the three Older Girls were packed up and dropped off to spend a week at Camp Findley, a church-run camp a couple of hours away on a small lake. I was probably about eight years old. We were each assigned a bunk in a cabin with other girls our age. I didn't know anyone in my cabin.

To this day, this event stands out as my first traumatic event. It was too much for me. I had never been away from home (except when all six kids and Mom went to visit grandparents for a week every summer), and now I was separated from my parents AND sisters?

I began crying. The crying quickly grew into huge, hysterical, inconsolable sobs. I couldn't stop and the poor counselors couldn't calm me down. You would think eventually I'd cry myself out and settle down, but I didn't. I couldn't.

They finally found one of my sisters and brought her to me. Yes, that calmed me down. Eventually, I settled in for the week.

As an adult, I have thought about this early memory. I now identify that the powerful emotion that would not go away that day was *abandonment*. I felt like an astronaut doing a space walk – outside and away from the relative safety of being inside the space ship. The astronaut is only safe as long as the tether is secure. I did not have a tether as far as I could tell. I was on a free-fall in outer space.

I have since learned that for a child, leaving home is only as safe as the child's sense of security with the parents. At that time in my life, there had been enough experience for me to feel that there was no secure connection—no tether—so I panicked. Like the movie *Gravity*, I was the astronaut whose tether was cut off from the safety of home. There was no secure connection for me at all.

At the end of the week, Mom and Dad arrived to pick us up. The counselors pulled my parents aside to tell them about my hysterical crying and that one of my sisters had finally been able to calm me. If ever there was a time when I needed some comforting words, this was it. But no comforting words came. Not this day. Not ever.

Instead what I heard were my father's words: "You big BABY." He looked at me and spit out the awful words. With contempt.

Did he view it as a reflection on him? Did I make him look bad? I still try to make sense of it.

From that day on, I knew I was right about one thing. I was alone in the world. Whatever happened, I was on my own.

But I had heard something at that church camp. I had clearly heard the gospel. Sunday School was mostly about learning famous Bible stories, and applications were mostly moral lessons. Be good. Don't lie. Be kind to others.

But church camp was intentional about spelling out the gospel to children.

> *God loved me. But I was a sinner (I knew this was true). Because God loved me so much, He willingly sent His Son Jesus to earth where He died on the cross to pay for my sins. But in order to make this sacrifice count for me, I had to accept it. It was a free gift, but until I received the gift, it wasn't mine.*

Each evening there was a lively service with fun music and then a short sermon. And at the end of each night, there was always an altar call. The preacher pleaded with the children to stand up, leave their seats, walk down the aisle to the front, where we could pray for salvation. Each evening, several children did just that.

I thought about it. I really did. But there was a lot of emotion swirling around that room, and I did not want to do something that was based on nothing more than emotion. If I ever did this—accept God's free gift—it would have to be a decision I made. If I did it, I knew it would change everything.

> *See God's fingerprints? There was a scholarship fund to pay our way to summer camp. And I heard the gospel clearly for*

the first time. God's plan to
reach me was in motion.

Back home, the rhythm of life continued. I reached my teens without any real issues. Those Sunday School lessons continued, but with no real impact. No one my age lived a life any different than my own. Oh well. Maybe someday I'd figure it out.

I thrived in school. That seemed to be a place where I could shine. Nearly every report card showed that I was on the honor roll.

And then there was that day. I did not see this coming. Not at all.

CHAPTER 3

Completely unexpectedly, there was **THAT** day. The day that just changed my whole world. For the rest of my life, time was divided in two: before that day, and after that day. I think I was about fifteen years old.

It was Sunday, so we had gone to Sunday School, and just like always, as soon as we got home we went to our bedrooms to change into play clothes. We four sisters shared a bedroom, and on this day, I was the last one in the room. Get into play clothes and run outside to play. That's what we always did.

Suddenly, without warning, I just knew… that God was in the room with me!

It was not scary; it was just very real. His very real Presence filled the space. And then, quietly, in my soul, I heard a single word:

Choose.

That was it. Just one single word. I knew immediately what He meant. I was standing at a fork in the road. The path my life had taken so far was now divided into two paths. I had to choose: would I continue down the path I'd walked every day of my life? Or… would I turn aside to head down a brand new, different path?

I'd been dodging the idea for a few years by then. Receiving the gift of salvation was something I actually liked; I did think I would do that. *Someday*. Maybe when I was "old." I mean, I didn't know a single person who had done this. Other than the Sunday School teachers (none of whom I had any connection with), no kids that I knew had done this. So what difference would it make? Seriously?

Not knowing what difference it would make was the reason it had always been so easy to push it aside. Maybe it would all make sense to me when I was older and wiser. In the meantime, kids are supposed to have fun, right? And even I knew, as a teen, "fun" would probably mean occasionally crossing over the line into outright sin. Everyone did that. No big deal. Right?

But I also knew that if and when I decided to accept God's gift of salvation, it would change everything. I am not sure how I knew that; I just did. Intentional, habitual sin would have to go. Little lies. Big lies. Mean, hateful thoughts. It would have to go.

But here He was! Asking me to make that choice. NOW. I could see my life laid out in a path before me. The path at my feet branched out into two distinct directions. This really was a fork in the road. Would I continue down the do-as-I-please path? That's what everyone else did.

Or would I turn aside and start a whole new adventure following Jesus?

And in a moment, I said YES to Him!

See God's fingerprints? When He knew it was time, He came to me! He knew me; He loved me. And He wanted me! He knew ahead of time that I would need Him through the coming years.

1

That moment still stands as fresh in my mind today as it was that day many decades ago. I never regretted the decision I made that day. Ever.

I finished changing into play clothes and ran downstairs. I didn't tell my sisters. I didn't tell my parents. I didn't tell anyone. There wasn't anyone to tell. No one in the whole world knew.

Except God. God knew! Somehow, in that moment, He became my Father. And as time passed, my Heavenly Father became more and more real to me, filling the void my earthly father never had.

And then slowly, almost imperceptibly, my life began to change. Tiny, baby steps at first. I asked for a Bible for Christmas, a gift that I treasured. Even though the archaic language of the King James Version made little sense to me, it still seemed sacred, and I began to watch for opportunities to be alone in our shared bedroom (four sisters in one room). I wanted to open this Good Book and read it.

Why was I drawn to this Book? A lot of it didn't make much sense to me, but there were nuggets that did. I know now that the Holy Bible is God's own inspired Word.

I had no idea how my decision that day to turn aside from the path I was on would actually change everything. How could I have known? It was all baby steps.

*See God's fingerprints? He
prompted me to get a Bible.
He drew me to the sacred
words in that Bible.*

CHAPTER 4

Ordinary life went on. I finished high school and had no idea what to do next. Somehow, all six of us kids just sort of knew that once we were through high school, it was time to leave the nest. We were on our own. I don't know how we knew that; we just did.

The word "college" was never even spoken. Clearly, obviously, there was no money and no one from my family had ever gone to college. My two older sisters had found their way working in business. Both had left Bradford, Pennsylvania and moved to Rochester, New York where good jobs were more plentiful. And, of course, more options for single adults to have fun.

After high school, I really had no idea what I wanted to do next. I was tired of school; I knew that much. I never even took the college entrance exam (SAT). Why would I?

Initially, I took a job as a clerical office worker for a small manufacturing company in Bradford. It paid me minimum wage, which at that time was $1.40 per hour.

Having a full time job meant I had my own money. That also meant paying rent to Mom and Dad. In my first real job, I answered phones, typed letters, and filed. *yawn* It didn't take long for me to realize this was not something I wanted to do for long. The boredom factor convinced me of that. I also kept working my part-time job at McCrory's Five and Ten Cent store where I had worked part-time since I turned sixteen. I ran the cash register and stocked shelves.

Finally, after six months I enrolled in a computer programming school located in Pittsburgh (Electronic Computer Programming Institute – ECPI). The entrance exam showed that I had a strong aptitude for computer programming. Loans were available, and I signed all the papers so I could pay it all back after graduating.

This launched me out of my parents' home. I was filled with a mixture of excitement and trepidation. My father drove me the three hours to deposit me alone in a strange big city. I was completely alone.

I stayed downtown in a six-story women's dorm run by the YWCA. It was only two blocks from my school, and their cafeteria served three meals a day, so it was perfect. My assigned roommate was a student enrolled in another business school. We got along great. She left each weekend to travel home, but that was not an option for me.

I understood that it was all on me to make this work. My first few days were spent searching for a part-time job. I needed enough income to pay for shampoo, soap, and personal items. In the first few days, I landed the perfect job. ECPI (my school) hired me to work in the office from 1:00 to 5:00. My classes were 8:00 to noon, Monday through Friday. That meant I would have to complete the homework assignments in the evenings.

> *God definitely opened doors*
> *for me to land this perfect job*
> *with enough hours to earn the*
> *income I needed, with no*
> *conflict of work/school*
> *schedule.*

During my six months there, only once did I take a Greyhound bus to travel back home for a weekend visit, but that was such a long, slow trip (stopping at every little town), despite feeling homesick, I never did it again.

Alone on the weekends, I searched for a church I could attend and found one within walking distance, just three blocks away. Only now, looking back, I realize clearly it wasn't even close to a Bible-teaching, evangelical, gospel-centered church. Back then, I didn't know the difference, but honestly, the classic hymns were filled with worship and biblical truth. I soaked that in. The sermon? Not so much. Mostly just be good; be kind; be generous.

See God's hand here? He opened up the school opportunity for me to learn computer programming. He showed me how to pay for it via loans. He helped me find a church.

CHAPTER 5

Six months later, I graduated from ECPI, first in my class.

After graduating, it was time to figure out where I wanted to live and then find a job, ASAP. It was my responsibility to put a roof over my head, food on the table, and then start paying back the school loan.

I moved to Rochester, New York, to join my two older sisters. They lived together in a one-bedroom apartment; they offered me the couch. That worked long enough for me to find a job and start earning money, which I did fairly quickly.

By this time, my sisters had plunged into the nightlife available to young singles in a metropolitan area. I soon learned that "nightlife" meant "bars." They were fully embracing it all and went out four nights a week (Friday, Saturday, Sunday, and Wednesday). I stayed at home alone, preferring to read. We didn't even have a TV.

The apartment was actually a cute little space on the back side of what had once been a large, beautiful home in a nice area. Now divided into two units, we had an outdoor stairway to the second floor apartment door that opened into the living room. The kitchen and bathroom were also on this floor. The lone bedroom was on the third floor and was actually a finished section of the attic. It worked out fine, except it was really hot in the summer with no air-conditioning. The bus stop was just a few doors away; I took buses everywhere I went.

As soon as I moved to Rochester, I wanted to find a church. My heart was still longing to learn more about this God I now belonged to. Of course, I needed to find a church that would be accessible on the bus line. My sisters urged me to go to the big Third Presbyterian Church only a few miles away (they had been there once), so that's where I went. This church drew musical talent from the highly renowned Eastman School of Music, and I loved that. The music itself fed my soul.

Soon enough, I decided to take a big, scary step and see if I could join the choir. I loved to sing, and I was captivated by the angelic music this choir produced. One small problem: joining this choir required that I pass an audition.

I decided to try. Singing solo anyplace anywhere is one of the scariest things in life for me, but if I never tried, I would never know. So I scheduled an audition, did my best, and to my surprise, I made it! They allowed me to join this beautiful choir. So one evening a week, I went for rehearsal, and each Sunday morning I arrived early to put on a choir robe and sing heavenly, worshipful music. Though the sermon was not Bible teaching, and the theology was definitely liberal, I didn't know any of that back then. So in the end, it was the music itself that fed my soul.

> *See God's fingerprints here? This liberal church was actually a stepping stone to the Bible-teaching church God wanted for me.*

Several months went by this way until one day the strangest thing happened. During the ten-minute break midway through choir rehearsal, one of the ministers on staff stopped by the choir room and called me over for a private conversation. Prior to this, I'd never even had a conversation with him. He gently and kindly told me that maybe I'd like it better at another church across town.

What??!!

A minister was actually urging me to leave his church? He told me to try Brighton Community Church, which, it turns out, was a great gospel-centered, Bible-teaching church that even had a vibrant group of young single adults!

This changed my whole world.

I did indeed visit this church. And I never left. The solid Bible teaching was food for my soul. I drank it in. The active singles group was a safe place for me to make friends and even more importantly – to see what it looks like to actually live the life of a person totally committed to following Jesus. Girlfriends were important, and I even dated some of the guys.

> *See God's fingerprints here? Finally I was in the church God wanted for me.*

It was at this church that I first heard of baptism. And it wasn't just any kind of baptism. They did complete immersion baptism. Well, for a person with a fear of water, this was terrifying to me. But as I learned that submitting to baptism is something every follower of Jesus does, I signed up. Fear or no fear, I was going to do it.

So one Sunday evening, in front of several hundred people, I went into the baptistry at the front of the sanctuary and affirmed my personal faith in Jesus. And then I went under the water.

The symbolism is so powerful: buried with Him in baptism, raised with Him into new life. My baptism was a tangible, concrete expression of my faith. It was a very meaningful day and meant a lot to me. I did it alone. I'm not sure I even invited my sisters to come. I don't remember. By now, I was so used to being alone; it was okay.

> *See God's fingerprints here?*
> *Following God's clear leading to*
> *immersion baptism was actually an*
> *opportunity for me to demonstrate that*
> *my faith was real.*

Brighton Community Church became my "second home." They also had an awesome library of Christian books that I could borrow. I read some of the giants of the faith. For a person who loves to read, this was like pure gold to me!

This was where I first learned about the story of George Mueller. Then there was Brother Andrew and his book, *God's Smuggler*. I read Hannah Whitall Smith's book, *The Christian's Secret to a Happy Life*. These giants in the faith became mentors to me.

> *See God's fingerprints here? As a*
> *person who loves to read, this church*
> *with a great library really did change*
> *my life.*

Like a dry, thirsty sponge, I soaked up every lesson I could. The first time I heard about tithing, I just did it. Anything that was taught in the Bible, I was ready to do.

Tithing was a habit I began then and never stopped, even during some very lean seasons in my life. From that day to this, I have never missed giving the first 10% of my income to my local church.

I also volunteered as a helper in the kindergarten class Sunday mornings. I could help during one service, and then attend the worship service during the second hour. I knew I couldn't teach a class; I didn't know enough myself to teach. But I could help out, and even this helped me grow.

There's nothing like a dry sponge when it finally lands in water! And that's exactly what I felt like during those early years.

I learned how important it was to memorize some key Bible verses. I even remember the very first verse I ever learned: 1 Corinthians 10:13. For a new believer it was a great verse to know.

> *"No temptation has overtaken you except what is common to mankind. And God is faithful; he will not let you be tempted beyond what you can bear. But when you are tempted, he will also provide a way out so that you can endure it."*

I've never found it easy to memorize, but if memorizing Bible verses was important, then that's what I'm going to do. I learned some basic verses to explain the gospel. I wanted to learn. I wanted God to use me.

As my new faith grew, I locked in what became my life goal: to glorify God and serve Him.

At some point, I began to sense a calling on my life. This seemed like a stretch for me, but I had a growing sense that God was going to make me a pastor's wife.

Me? A pastor's wife? Wow...

> *See God's fingerprints here? Tithing and baptism were early ways I demonstrated my intention to follow Jesus. Memorizing Bible verses was another really important discipline I learned.*

CHAPTER 6

One weekend, we three sisters traveled back to Bradford to visit our parents. I have a very distinct memory from this one visit. I have told this memory to Mickey, but I don't think I ever told anyone else, nor have I written it down anywhere.

For some reason (I don't know why), we all went out to dinner together. Uncle Harold joined us for this dinner and I was seated close enough to overhear this conversation.

Uncle Harold was talking to our father. He said something like, "You know how kids are. Those girls (motioning to the three of us) are going out, living the party lifestyle up there in Rochester." It was an easy assumption for these two atheist brothers to make.

But then my dad said words I will never forget. Pointing at me, he said, "Not this one. She's different."

That was it. I was shocked at hearing these words. Yes, it was absolutely true – I was different, but how did my dad know that? We didn't talk to him about anything, ever! So what did he see in me that made me look different than my sisters? I have no idea. I wish I knew. But as the years and then decades have passed, I never forgot that comment.

Eventually, I concluded that even a hard-hearted atheist could see some fruit of the Spirit. Something was visible. In the end I just thanked God that my early, clumsy life as a baby Christian was visible in some way.

> *See God's fingerprints here? In a seemingly random, casual family dinner, God planted me close enough to my dad and uncle to be able to overhear this conversation. As the years passed, this memory became very dear to me. It was something I thanked God for.*

Back to life in Rochester, my life from that living room couch was pretty routine. One might even say "boring." I worked 40 hours/week, came home, fixed a simple meal, read, and went to bed. Sunday mornings I went to church. That was truly a highlight in my week. Sunday evenings the young single adults from my new church got together; it was part social and part teaching time.

One hot, summer Friday night, I was home alone in the second floor apartment. My sisters had gone out. Because it was so stifling hot, even the fan didn't help much. I read until I was sleepy, and then I made up my couch-bed with a sheet, turned off the lights, and tried to sleep in the heat. At some point, I heard footsteps coming up the outdoor stairs, and then the door opened into the living room. I was right across the room on the couch. At that time, we did not lock the door until everyone was home for the night.

Instantly, I saw that it was a strange man who had just walked in. Who was this? And why was he here? What could have brought him here?

I froze, hoping he wouldn't notice me in the dim light. But there was enough light for him to see me, and he walked right over to me.

Me...with very little clothing on. Wearing just super light cotton shorty pajamas. Suddenly feeling terribly exposed, I reached for the thin sheet and tried to cover myself. He just smiled and crouched down beside me. Just inches away, I could smell the alcohol on his breath. At first he made meaningless small talk, but very soon he just began touching me. *All over.*

Terrified, I realized I might be raped. With no sisters home yet, and with no idea if anyone would hear me if I screamed, I tried to remain calm. He told me he was there because he had ridden with his friend, who was still downstairs in the car with one of my sisters. He was clearly drunk.

This whole experience was traumatizing for me. I had zero actual experience with sex, and now I was going to lose my virginity like this? I was horrified, scared, and revolted at the very thought.

Please God, I need help!

Suddenly, without warning, this drunk stranger stood up and walked back to the door, saying something about checking on his friend. As soon as he was out, I leaped up, ran across the room, and bolted the door. No one – even with a key – would get in unless I opened the bolt.

> *In the midst of a potentially life-altering, scary scenario, I called on God to help me… and He did!*

Only a minute or two later, this stranger was back. He obviously expected to walk right back in and was pretty mad when he found the door was locked and bolted. He yelled at me through the locked door. "Your sister is sick. She needs to get in." I told him I would open the door only WHEN my sister was at the door.

That night ended with God answering my panicked prayer. That might have been the first time I saw God very specifically answer prayer for me. He really did respond to my desperate call for help.

One Friday, one of my sisters was tired of seeing me stuck in that hot, boring apartment every weekend. She was having a blast discovering Rochester's nightlife. She begged and pleaded with me to join her and other friends for a "fun, exciting night out on the town." Finally, I relented. After all, what did I know? I had never gone "out on the town." She told me there would be music and dancing. It would be fun!

Well, I liked to dance! So, against my better judgment, I relented, and off we went. I don't remember who had a car, but we were all together in one car.

The place was jam packed with young, single adults. There was a bar, and people were drinking and some were dancing. It was very crowded, making it hard to avoid some body-rubbing. I was immediately uncomfortable in this space. A few times a guy asked me to dance. But the overall sense was that this was a meat-market, intended for people to meet others. I did indeed feel like a piece of meat, part of a line of steaks – just a piece of meat to be consumed. Both men and women were checking each other out, looking for a dance, a date, or maybe even a hook-up for the night. Just one slow dance made me want to find a shower.

I was horrified.

And I had no way out. Until the people I'd ridden with were ready to go, I was stuck in this place.

It finally ended. We went home. That was enough for me.

This was what the fuss was all about? This was what my sisters loved so much? It was creepy to me. I never went back.

Even though I had graduated #1 in my class at ECPI, it was hard to find an entry-level job as a computer programmer. The world of computers was just emerging.

I needed income, so when I first moved to Rochester, I took a job working at a bank in their computer processing department. It was a paycheck.

This was many years before personal computers. Each company invested in large, bulky machines (mainframe computers), along with large disk drives and tape drives. The computers took up an entire room. If a company was investing in computers, they needed to hire their own programmers. There were no software packages you could just buy.

All data input was done via keypunch machines where keypunch operators "typed" in data, causing the machines to punch holes in a code format that would be readable to the machines.

Reading lines of data and keying it into this machine created a card with holes punched out.

Keypunch card

I did various things in that job for about ten months, when I finally landed a job as a computer programmer at a small local manufacturing company. I was the second (backup) programmer. At least here, I was actually building a resume.

All went well for a while. But then, slowly, I realized that the Vice President of the company had his eye on me. At first I was flattered, thinking he might promote me, give me a raise, or something honorable. I was still the small town girl with a high level of naiveté.

However, it soon became apparent that nothing honorable was going to happen. With a big smile on his face one day, he told me that his wife was out of town for a week, and he wondered if I would like to see his home?

I quickly found another job.

This time, it was a job I was proud of. I was joining a team of six computer programmers at Rochester Institute of Technology (RIT). The people were nice, professional, and the team patiently helped me learn the ropes.

This job paid enough for me to be able to buy a car. My first car! However, until I found one, I continued riding the public bus to and from work.

At the end of one work day, I rode the elevator down to the first floor to catch the bus home. I was shocked to see a man with a big smile on his face waiting for me as the elevator door opened. It was the Vice President from my previous job. He offered me a ride, "so I didn't have to take the bus."

I hastily declined and got on that bus as quickly as I could.

> *God was still with me, protecting me from a potentially scary situation.*

Shortly after that, I did buy my first car. It was a Volkswagen beetle convertible, with a stick shift. I didn't even know how to drive a stick shift yet, but I figured I could learn! It was a cheap car and got great gas mileage, so it worked for me.

But that programming job at RIT? It was not what I imagined. This time my problem was the boredom factor. Sitting most of the day alone in a little cubicle, writing code, running my programs, debugging them... over and over.

I began to see that this was not a good career choice for me. I knew I had the aptitude for it, the pay was good, and I was getting good performance reviews, but it sort of made me go a little crazy. Having an aptitude for it didn't necessarily mean it was a good fit for me.

What next? What was I to do?

See God's fingerprints here? Even at RIT, God showed me that this job was not going to be my landing place.

CHAPTER 7

College? Me? Not one person from my family had ever gone to college. Some, including my dad, had not even finished high school. That was not uncommon back then, growing up in a very rural small town in the hills of Pennsylvania.

A couple of the men I had met at Brighton Community Church had graduated from Roberts Wesleyan College, a Christian college located on the west side of Rochester. With my increasing awareness that computer programming was not going to work for me long term, I began to think about going to college. This was a huge step for me. I also knew I would have to finance it and pay for it completely on my own.

But the more I thought about it, the more I liked it. By this time, I had learned that I could make adult, responsible decisions, and if I decided college was a good plan, then I'd find a way to pay for school. And I was also learning that I could count on God to guide me.

Maybe I would pursue a teaching career. I began to move forward. I had lived in New York state long enough to qualify for in-state financing (which was cheaper) and was able to qualify for some grants and some loans. By this time, I had been out of high school for three years. I had not even bothered to take the SAT exam while I was in high school. Why would I? That was for people headed for college. So I even had to find out where and how to register for the SAT.

I figured out the whole application process, was accepted to the school, resigned from my programming job at RIT, sold my car, and moved into a dorm on campus.

See God's fingerprints here? I was learning to trust God to guide me as I explored ideas and moved forward. I was going to college!

College was another completely new environment for me. I had been working and living in the world of independent adults for three years now, and the rest of the incoming freshman class seemed very young to me. They had not yet launched from their parents' home.

But it was a Christian college and I was more than ready to live in a Christian environment. On the first day there, standing in line for registration, it became apparent that most people were here with friends from high school. I knew no one. But it turned out that the person right next to me in line was also here with no roommate. We hit it off right away and decided to room together. Patty's high school boyfriend was also enrolling, but she had no girlfriends enrolling.

Slowly I made friends and even dated some of the guys. Guess what? Some of the guys at this college were training to become... pastors.

I wasn't really interested in marriage. Not yet. I wanted to pursue this dream of graduating from college.

Me! A college graduate! Who could imagine it?

So my dates were not serious. It was casual dating, meeting and making new friends. Eventually I was asked out by the man I did end up marrying ("George[2]"). He was a ministerial student with plans to become a pastor. When I arrived as a freshman, he was a junior. Sort of a big-man-on-campus, he was the Vice President of the Student Body, which, it turns out, meant that he functioned as the temporary President of the new freshman class until we were ready to elect our own officers. That's how we met.

---

[2] Name changed

We dated for a while, but it soon became apparent that he was increasingly much more into me than I was into him. He was clearly on a serious, maybe-marriage track, and that was not my track, so eventually I gently told him it was over.

I thought that was that. I dated a few other guys – friends, casual, fun dates. One of them, however, let me in on a little secret. George had made it known that he still wanted me. And somehow other guys who wanted to date me… were supposed to ask George for permission first!

I was appalled. This just wasn't right. It was just really, really wrong on so many levels.

Eventually, we did reconnect. It was the summer before my second year and before his senior year. I spent the summer on campus after landing a 40-hour-per-week job working in the office.

My heart was yearning for spiritual renewal on campus. By the time I'd been there a full year, it was apparent to me that many – maybe even most – students were either not Christians at all, or else were very immature, cultural Christians still riding on their parents' apron strings. I was learning. Maybe growing up in a Christian home had some inherent dangers of its own.

It was this yearning that prompted me to reach out to George. He was training for ministry; surely spiritual renewal was an issue we would agree on. I was hoping for some strategy planning. Instead, we ended up dating again. A few months later, he proposed, and I accepted.

Marrying him would mean I would be a pastor's wife. It all seemed to fit. I longed to create a family that would serve Christ. I longed to be a mother and raise my kids to know and love the great God I had so fallen for.

What could go wrong?

It turns out… a lot.

Were there red flags? Yes, absolutely. But the red flags were only visible to me many years later. At the time, I was still so young and naïve. I did not recognize any red flags.

One red flag I wish I had recognized was this: Part of my fantasy-dream of being in a Christian marriage included reading the Bible together and praying together. That would definitely be a new experience for me, but I had heard that this is a good thing for Christians to do.

So one day, I suggested we do this. So… we did.

Problem was… it was weird. Just totally awkward. It just didn't work. I didn't know how to make it work. It was all new to me. I'd hoped to find a way for the two of us to be able to read from the Bible together and pray together.

Simple, right? I thought it was a basic thing to do, especially for Christians who were serious about living out their faith. Was it wrong for me to expect this from a person planning to be a pastor?

No. Even now I don't think it was expecting too much. I think I was right about that. The fact that we couldn't make this happen should have been a huge red flag. We were completely unable to make it happen. Eventually, we just gave up trying.

That should have been the end of it. The end of us.

As I write this now, many, many years later, some things become clear. I have now been happily married to Mickey for thirteen years, so speaking with some experience, I realize that reading the Bible together and praying together is a very intimate, vulnerable, transparent thing to do.

But here's the difference: Mickey and I do it easily.

The failure to accomplish this seemingly small simple task should have been a huge warning sign to me. But I didn't know that then.

See God's fingerprints here? He prompted me to leave behind the computer programming career and enroll in college. He provided funds to pay for college. And putting me in the right place at the right time, I met the woman who ended up being my roommate.

CHAPTER 8

We married in August the summer after George graduated. The plan was to move to Kansas City, where he would begin his three-year seminary training to become a pastor. My own plans to graduate from college were put on hold. I still wanted to earn that degree, but in my new role as wife, soon-to-be-pastor's wife, putting my plans on hold seemed like the right thing to do.

So, we married and moved a thousand miles away from family and friends. I worked full time; he worked part time, and for three years, we squeaked by.

As a fairly new follower of Jesus, my heart's desire was for the rest of my family to get to know this amazing God I loved so much. I decided to write a letter addressed to each of my five siblings and spouses. The letter was part my own story, and then I spelled out the basic gospel – good news. This was way before email, of course, so I made photocopies and snail-mailed a copy to each.

Sadly, I never heard back from any of them.

I landed a job working as an assistant computer programmer at a local bank. I was not a computer operator; that was a separate skill and not my forte. However, very soon the Vice President asked me to be the computer operator for just one task: payroll. Of course, this was a highly confidential process. Management always wants to protect any and all payroll records.

But, why me? Somehow the Vice President knew I could be trusted. I don't know how he knew he could trust me, but he was right. It seemed that God was again making my character visible in some way. It really was becoming second nature to me.

Married life was an entirely new thing. In what should have been a long honeymoon season for the two of us to adjust to marriage, it wasn't even close to that. Obviously, I can only speak for myself, but any expectations I had going into marriage just slowly evaporated.

With the passage of time, we seemed to develop parallel lives. Separate from each other.

I still looked forward to having babies and raising children. Clearly, I was not doing well as a wife. Maybe I could do better as a mom.

Three years later, after graduation from seminary, the new graduates began interviewing for jobs and beginning their professional careers in real pastoral work. George finally was offered a pastorate at a tiny church (about 50 people), and I took an office job part-time to help make ends meet. By now, we were ready to begin having babies, and after several months, I was finally pregnant. I continued working until the baby was born, and then I began my hardest job of all: being a full time, stay-at-home mom.

I actually did that job full time for about eighteen years. It was a job I completely loved. Yes, it was my most difficult job, but it was also the most rewarding.

Two more babies came along, keeping me totally busy. I actually loved being pregnant, and I loved being a mom.

God made my new nature visible to my employer. And then even with a difficult marriage, God remained close to me. As I continued reading the Bible, I learned more and more about Him. And then,

He did bless me with babies!

I did have one problem though: I was becoming seriously depressed. Probably clinically depressed. The marriage was also becoming more and more a huge problem for me. It was just… so, so empty.

CHAPTER 9

Gradually, I began to realize I was in serious trouble. My depression was not going away; it was getting worse. What was I to do?

We lived on a super skimpy bare-bones budget. I made most of my own clothes and many for the kids. There was no money for a therapist, and I was operating under the unspoken rule of pastor's wives:

Thou shalt always protect the public reputation of your pastor-husband.

Where did I learn that? Not sure, but maybe in the handful of meetings the seminary held for wives of the seminary students.

There was no way I felt free to tell anyone – anyone at all – the state of my marriage. Feeling very, very alone, I just did my best. I truly loved being a mom. At some point, I just shifted my focus to doing my best for my two sons (my daughter wasn't yet born).

Still, "doing my best" was not working. It became increasingly clear that *something* had to happen, or I was going to break. It was not hard for me to recognize this sad truth: I was hovering on a dangerously thin edge of a complete mental breakdown.

Nobody knew that. Nobody at all. And yet, it was true.

The single, lone thing that saved my sanity during this period was… my daily quiet moments spent in the presence of the living God, reading the Bible and praying. With a toddler and a baby to care for, I got the two of them on the same nap schedule as soon as possible. That nap time was my sacred opportunity to be with God. Nothing was more important than that.

> *See God's fingerprints here? My daily Bible reading was my lifeline at this time. God is so good; He used that thirty-minute window to nourish me.*

Why was this so important to me? Because during these thirty minutes, the dark cloud that completely surrounded me all day and all night – *that* dark cloud – just… disappeared. Every day during the time I was alone to meet with God – no dark cloud. That's why I couldn't afford to skip it. Not even for a day. It was my lifeline.

Every day, I would read a chapter or two from the Bible. Every day, I began where I left off the day before. I read, drinking in the truth of this Holy Book. And then I prayed. My prayers were becoming more and more desperate.

God, I really need Your help. I am not going to make it.

Honest words.

I couldn't stop my thoughts: Who would raise my kids? If I ended up institutionalized in a mental health facility, who would love them as much as I did?

No one! I absolutely knew that. I loved my kids so much. Please, God*! Please help me!*

> *Even in desperate times, I knew to turn to God for help. I stayed connected to Him.*

And then finally, there was… that day.

I just broke.

I could not continue this way anymore. I knew it. It was the end of the line.

Sitting quietly in the sweet, sweet presence of God, I read from the Bible. That's where He always spoke to me.

And then, as always, I searched for words to say back to Him.

But this day was different. At first, my prayer was just tears. I am not a crier by nature, so this flood of tears was completely out of character for me. And then finally... these words.

Okay, God, I give up. You know my heart. You know the only thing I want from life is to glorify You. I do not see any way for this sad, depressed life to glorify You.

I paused, took a deep breath and finally said these words.

Still, You know all that. So, if You can use even this depressed mom, living like this, then I yield it all to You. It makes no sense to me at all, but I am now giving up any claim to happiness.

I'm all Yours.

There. I'd said it. That was all I had to say.

And with that, I was done.

I closed my Bible, wiped my tears away and blew my nose. Then I sat quietly waiting for that nearly tangible, all-too-familiar dark cloud to come rolling back. It always did.

But ten minutes went by... no dark cloud.

Another half hour... still sunshine.

I didn't know what to make of this. I felt like holding my breath. I didn't want to do anything that might change it. I like the sunshine.

And with the passing of hours, and then days, it became clear.

My dark depression was GONE.

Completely gone.

But, I had not asked God to heal me! He just did! Slowly I began to put two and two together.

It was my complete surrender! That must have been what He wanted from me all along.

And to this day, the word "surrender" is a sweet sound to my soul.

I still love sunshine.

See God's fingerprints here? Even in this very dark season, I always knew that God still loved me. He stayed close to me. He fed my soul during my daily quiet moments with Him. And when it seemed the darkness would never end, He nudged me into surrender. When I did, God healed me!

CHAPTER 10

Life resumed. I became pregnant with my third (and last) child. That brought me joy. There was nothing in the whole world like carrying a tiny, growing baby inside. After two sons, I was happy to have a daughter. A beautiful, strawberry blond perfect baby girl.

So perfect.

And then of course, life really got crazy busy with an infant and two young boys.

God was good. I knew that. I had known that since I was fifteen. Long ago I had burned my bridges; the only way was forward. I was completely in love with the actual Creator of the entire Universe. It was amazing.

It was always amazing. I mean, I knew where I'd come from. I was just one more lost soul, in the middle of a messy batch of six very poor kids, all born within nine years. I was third of the six, and grew up feeling pretty much invisible. I was a lost child.

That's me on the right.
My scowling face!
This is where I came from.

That's why when I said YES to Jesus that day long ago, it changed my whole life. I was no longer lost! That meant everything to me. My Heavenly Father took the place my earthly father had never filled.

I finally had a Father.

See God's fingerprints here? He gave me a third pregnancy with a beautiful, healthy baby girl. He held me steady in the crazy days of raising three young children. And maybe most of all, He continued meeting with me every day.

I'm the one sitting on the floor, right side. With the birth of the sixth baby, the kids' ages were: 0, 1, 2, 6, 7, and 8.

CHAPTER 11

Along the way, I stayed pretty busy. As a stay-at-home mom, I also homeschooled the three kids up to about the fifth grade. So there were lesson plans to prepare, trips to the library for age-appropriate reading material, and lead the kids through their daily school work. And of course, a house to clean, groceries to buy, and meals to prepare.

Always interested in following news, I began paying more attention to the pro-life movement, created after abortion became legal via the U.S. Supreme Court *Roe v. Wade* decision in 1973. Eventually, I volunteered to serve on our own county-wide pro-life organization. I went to the monthly meetings, where I learned more. One year, I traveled with a group on a bus to Washington, D.C. for the annual March for Life held each year in January on the steps of the Supreme Court. It was a meaningful day for me.

During the early years of the pro-life movement, some organizations held protests in front of abortion clinics. There were no abortion clinics in our small town, so abortion-minded women generally went to Buffalo, New York to one of the many clinics there.

Our group decided to charter a bus for a day trip to one of the clinics, where we would peacefully hold signs, sing worship songs, and especially… pray.

I signed up.

We were advised on what to expect. There was always the possibility that local police would arrive and begin arresting people. We were told that being arrested was completely optional. It was a personal decision each individual was to make.

As expected, there was also a pro-abortion group gathered to protest us. The two groups were kept separate. When we needed a bathroom break, we would walk a block to McDonalds and then grab coffee or food.

Someone from our group decided to bring boxes of donuts back and delivered them to… the other side. Our group stayed peaceful, walking around, praying, and singing

"Our God is an Awesome God." It was eye-opening for me to notice the contrast between the two groups. Across the street were angry, yelling, sometimes including profanity, snarling people. We had been coached not to respond at all.

I realized that you could show pictures of the two groups to any random person, and anyone would know which side was pro-life and which was pro-abortion. It was actually pretty sad.

One year, our county organization decided to hold a community pro-life event as a way to educate people on the issue, and urge people to pray, and support pro-life politicians. I agreed to chair this event.

We solicited pastors from local churches to participate in a public way. We rented the only auditorium available for this non-sectarian event. I was able to get a speaker from Focus on the Family to headline the occasion.

I searched the Bible for various Bible verses that speak to the sanctity of human life, and printed them out. This was a key part of the event. Each pastor was given one of the verses to read to the audience. They lined up in single file, and without comment, one by one, they approached the microphone and read the words. God's Words. It was sacred and powerful.

We had two worshipful songs sung by talented, Christian soloists. We pledged our allegiance to the flag. We prayed together.

To create a lighter moment, I had a rocking chair placed alone on the stage, and an adorable little girl skipped out to sit on my lap. I opened a colorful, children's storybook and began to read. I wish I could remember what story I used. I only know it fit with the general theme.

Truly, participating in the national pro-life movement was meaningful to me.

Please, God – make it stop. Please.

CHAPTER 12

My increasingly tense marriage was clearly my biggest problem. By far. It just never got better. In fact, it grew steadily worse and worse.

After our second pastoral position ended in George being fired (by a political split within the church) – we were voted out and had nowhere to go. We were homeless. The house we had lived in for five years was owned by the church and provided to the pastor and family. Being voted out meant we were not only without income; we were also homeless.

With nowhere to go, we boxed up most of our belongings and all our furniture. A kind family offered to store our things in their garage. So we did. And then filled our station wagon with basic clothes, a few toys for the kids, and school books for the homeschool lessons. At the time, the kids were 7, 5, and 3 years old.

George did land a few interviews before we left, but nothing worked out. We were homeless for about six weeks.

Not wanting to impose too much on various family members, we tried to spread it around. We started out at one set of grandparents, then moved to another set, and then on to a week with one of my sisters and her husband. It was a lot for anyone to take in. A family of five, with no place to go.

Eventually, a ministry position opened up in the small town where George's mother and step-father lived. We had settled in their basement for the time, and this position sounded like something to pursue. The job was to serve as a chaplain for twenty hours per week at the county nursing home, and twenty hours at the small local hospital.

After several interviews, George was offered the job, and we settled in this small, rural town. I was no longer a "pastor's wife" but George was still in ministry. He still preached fairly often, primarily to fill in when our own pastor was away, or for any of the other small churches around town.

I jumped in to serve at our new church. I taught Sunday School classes, Vacation Bible School classes, coached Bible Quizzing for children and later for the teens. I also served on the youth council.

For all of these years, George refused to serve in any volunteer capacity. He would preach when any pastor was away for vacation. But if it wasn't out front preaching, he was not interested. I had privately urged him to do something – anything – to be a good example for our kids but he never did.

The marriage managed to limp along for about ten more years. Finally, somehow, the two of us agreed to see a marriage counselor. With nearly no money for this new expense, we found a counselor who was pretty cheap.

Maybe it's true. You get what you pay for.

During our initial session, the counselor asked each of us to define the problem. Why were we there? As I tried to find the words, I included this never-before-spoken sentence.

"I feel like he believes that ALL of the marriage problems are MY problems. I don't think he believes he has done anything wrong at all to contribute to the marriage problems. Fix Cindy; problem solved."

The counselor turned to George and asked him if this were true.

"Yep."

Didn't even have to think about it. It was clearly his deeply held belief. I was right on this one point, this one sticking point.

We didn't stay with this counselor very long. Neither of us could see any results.

This scenario was repeated at each of the three counselors we saw during the next few years. I would make that same statement to the new counselor, and George would affirm that it was true. Still true. He was completely dug in on the "fact" that he was such an amazing husband (apparently perfect, with nothing at all to improve).

> *God's hand was evident in getting at least this foundational truth out in the open, on the table.*

The final counselor we saw was smart enough to know no one could help someone who was already "perfect." So this counselor suggested I come alone next time. Which I did. And learned a lot. I continued going solo with this counselor for many months.

No one can change another person. I can only change myself. And since I wasn't doing well at all, I was highly motivated to learn and change. I was an emotional wreck. I was on the very slim edge of a complete nervous breakdown. Eventually, with wise counsel from this marriage counselor, we separated.

The reason for the separation? Well, I badly needed some physical space in order to work at regaining some emotional stability. My very clear goal was to stabilize myself so that I could resume focusing on the real goal: making this marriage work.

Separation brought me some relief. I no longer had to encounter George on a daily basis. I continued my weekly counseling appointments.

And then, I discovered a book that I devoured (*Boundaries*, by Cloud and Townsend). I read it cover-to-cover about a dozen times. Marked it up. Turned corners on lots of pages. Read it again. This book changed my life.

> *God's hand was evident in getting this book into my hands. Learning about boundaries was a major eye-opening concept for me to learn and then put it into practice.*

Slowly I learned that I had operated my whole life without any real solid boundaries. It was like having property that really did belong to me (my life), but with no clear boundary lines. The result? Anyone – neighbors, family, or friends – could do whatever they wanted in and around "my" property.

The image of my own property with clear boundaries (pictured like a white picket fence) made it easier for me to spot when someone was violating my boundaries. They would have to come inside my fence to plant the flowers they like, or paint my white fence... purple! Or come right inside my home and rearrange the furniture.

Wait! They can't do that!

And yet I had lived my whole life pretty much allowing people around me to do exactly that with MY life. It was true that I didn't LIKE it, but with no tools to draw on, I just allowed it. I needed the *Boundaries* book to sort this out for me, and learn to change the rules for my life.

To this day, I still review the boundaries principle regularly. I subscribe to Henry Cloud's free e-newsletter; I follow him on Facebook. I read every email; I read every one of his Facebook posts.

I continued doing everything I could think of to stretch and grow toward health. Emotional health, mental health.

Good people around me helped me a lot.

My spiritual journey during this time was a mixture of knowing that God loved me, and at the same time, I just felt dry. Empty. Wrung out. I went through the motions of living life in a loveless marriage. I did the best I could to manage the home, clean the house, do the laundry, cook meals, and parent the kids. It was a sad time.

I also continued my intention not to bring the kids into what was an adult situation, especially one they had no control over. Because I loved my kids so much, I really wanted them to have a good relationship with their dad. I tried to create scenarios for the kids to connect.

I remember creating opportunities for the kids to foster connections with their dad. For example, from the time the kids were very young, when I heard George pull into the driveway after work, I yelled out to the kids, "Daddy's home! Daddy's home!" They learned to stop what they were doing and run to the door to greet him with a lot of noise, hugs, and love.

I actually did the same thing when my oldest child left home to attend school. When he arrived home, we all yelled his name and celebrated the fact that he was home.

After the separation, I learned that George was not playing by the rules. As I tried to protect the kids from any negative thoughts about their dad, I learned that this was not being reciprocated. That was hard. Really hard.

I had steadfastly maintained my intention not to allow a single person in the whole world to know what this marriage was really like on the inside. Protecting George's public reputation was something I felt responsible for. This was another one of my mistakes. I should have found at least one safe person to confide in. Better yet, two or three.

Confiding in no one may have been my biggest mistake. By the time I was telling this story to a professional counselor, I was a wreck. Having a girlfriend or two to confide in might have validated my experience. I might have even taken steps earlier when change might have had a chance.

Here's one huge thing I learned: It is not acceptable to treat me badly. It's just not. I began to repeat this mantra to myself:

Treat me well, or not at all.

I was the one who taught George that treating me badly was acceptable. I did that.

Now I just made up my mind. For the rest of my life, treating me well would be the only choice for anyone who wants to be in my life. If I realize I am being treated badly, it's up to me to make a clear, gentle request. *Your choice: treat me well, or not at all.* That meant I was back in charge of my own life. I don't yield control of my life to… anyone. It's really a basic boundary issue.

So if George wants back into my life, he will have to treat me well. Which would mean making changes. And of course, no one makes changes unless and until… they acknowledge that they have behavior that doesn't work. For George, that never happened.

It would mean confession. Repentance. Apologies.

If George's behavior and words consistently tell me that he intends to change nothing and I agree to stay, I would have to agree to continue being treated badly.

It's up to me to exit, if that's what it takes. And of course, eventually, that's what I did. Problem was it took me so long. Decades. By then a lot of patterns were set in concrete.

> *Clearly, God was intimately involved in guiding me and protecting me during this time. He was close to me! And I knew I could call on Him at any time. He never failed me.*

With no hope for anything better, I lowered my goals. Just tolerate this sad life. If I could do that, it would be okay. Just that. At the time, that seemed doable. It was the best I could hope for. I told myself I could do this.

But that was just not true. I should have faced the truth, and the earlier I did that, the better the outcome.

Eventually, of course, it all fell apart. My strategy failed. Turns out I was not able to survive the increasing pressure that seemed to be aimed at breaking me. Even after the separation.

The breaking worked.

Sometimes a day comes that I could never have seen coming. One of "those" days was about to land right in my lap.

It was probably good that I didn't see it coming.

CHAPTER 13

Through all of this, my daily quiet time with God was my lifeline. My counselor (a Christian) advised me to read through the Psalms. He thought it would help me process emotions. So I did. This turned out to be a much bigger part of my healing than I could have anticipated.

It made sense. Part of my previous coping strategies was to lock out emotions. It was probably a bad strategy that would never work long term, but I didn't know that. It worked for one day at a time. I just didn't allow myself to feel. I rarely cried.

Until this season of life. This whole season.

During this time, I knew I needed enough sanity to stay employed. My emotional pain was always just under the surface. My daily pattern was to just get through the day at work, escape out the back door of my office, and try to make it home to my little apartment (five minutes) before the dam of tears burst out again. When I made it to the safety of my new apartment, I got my Bible, sat on the floor beside the bed, and opened to where I'd left off the day before.

Why the floor? I don't know, except that's where I wanted – or needed – to be. Perhaps it was part of expressing my feelings. I was feeling very low, so sitting on the floor just felt right.

Sit in a comfortable chair? No. That's what normal people do.

So I began with the first Psalm and read one or two each evening, beginning where I left off the day before. I would read the words and then try to pray. For many weeks, my daily prayers consisted only of my desperate plea: *"Help me!"* That was all I could get out before the tears flowed again. Somehow I knew God was okay with that. It was raw. Authentic. Reading through the Psalms was definitely accomplishing the goal of unlocking my emotions.

It was a good plan. Every day, a few more Psalms followed by heartfelt, desperate prayer. An ocean of tears. I had an image in my mind as I sat on the floor beside my bed with my Bible open.

> *I see my Heavenly Father sitting in a rocking chair. When He sees me, He opens His arms, inviting me to join Him. I crawl up onto His lap and into His arms. He wraps His strong arms around me, holds me close, and just rocks me. It's a safe place. I let the tears flow and He just rocks me. Silently.*
>
> *He holds me close and just rocks me.*

This is an image that I never actually had in real life. There are no memories at all of anyone pulling me onto a lap to be rocked and comforted. Not my mother, not my father, not a grandma, not an aunt or uncle. No one. It is a void I felt keenly. I never saw this happen for any of my five siblings either.

But now, this daily ritual was again a lifeline for me. I knew God was real. I knew He cared. I knew He loved me. It was enough.

One day at a time.

> *It's amazing to me that I never doubted God's existence for a moment. I never doubted that He was real and that He cared for me.*

Every day, I just began reading where I'd left off the day before.

Until... the day I got to Psalm 34 and stopped at this verse.

> *"The Lord is close to the brokenhearted and saves those who are crushed in spirit."*

Is this true? Is the Lord close to the brokenhearted?
Brokenhearted? Wait... that's ME.

Was there ever a person more brokenhearted than I? And if this verse is true (and of course, it is), then it's also true that *He will save me*!

My tears instantly changed into tears of JOY!

It's true! This is true! The Lord is close!

I relaxed. It was not a total cure, but it sure felt good. Just for a moment, I rested in His care.

There was just a taste of... peace.

Wow... peace and joy. Seriously? Amazing.

A... MAZ... ING!

> *This was a life-changing moment for me. After this, everything was different. I knew it was true. And after the prolonged time of grief and despair, having even a moment of JOY and then PEACE was unexpected and loved.*

This one verse just stopped me in my tracks. I read it over and over. I couldn't move on.

And still, in this moment, my Heavenly Father is filling this void! How can this be true? And yet, it is. It is very true. I am content for this one moment, being held close by my Heavenly Father. My messy, blubbering, broken self, held close in His strong arms.

Amazing. It truly was amazing.

The next day, I arrived home, found my usual spot on the floor next to my bed and opened my Bible. Thinking I would perhaps read Psalm 34:18 again and then move on.

So that's what I did. I read it again.

But I couldn't move on. I just couldn't. I read that verse again and began gushing tears all over again.

"The LORD is close to the brokenhearted and saves those who are crushed in spirit."

I knew it was true. Long ago I had settled the fact that the Bible is divinely inspired and every verse is true.

It is true: God is close to me! I was so broken, but God was close!

My weeping was a mixture of profound brokenness and profound, deep joy at the truth of this verse. Both are true. I was profoundly broken, and God was close. I held both of these truths close. Like two sides of a coin, they were both true.

So I read the verse again. And just let the tears spill. And again my best attempt at prayer: *"God, help me."*

When the third day was another repeat, I gave up. I just settled into it. No longer fighting the impulse, I just stayed stuck on this one verse for many, many days. Read it, sobbed, and knew it was true. I crawled up onto the lap of my Father and let Him wrap His strong arms around me.

Peace.

Joy!

> *God guided me to Christian counselors when I needed professional help.*
>
> *He met with me as I opened my Bible each day.*
>
> *In the midst of profound emotional breakdown, He held me steady.*
>
> *He brought me to the verse I needed at just the right time (Psalm 34:18).*
>
> *In the worst time of my life, He not only wrapped His strong arms around me, He also gave me moments of peace and joy!*

CHAPTER 14

Eventually, of course, I was able to move on. I did finish
reading through the Psalms and found some relief as I read
the sacred words. Like a balm for my soul. God was good to
me. Even though I had to plow forward one day at a time,
God never left me to do any of it alone.

For sure, I had some hard work to do. With the help of
my counselor, some groups, and some solid reading, I had to
figure out what I had done wrong.

How had I gotten myself into this whole situation?
What, exactly, had I done that charted out my path to this
place? I needed to figure that out.

I continued those weekly counseling sessions. The
counselor taught me that you can't help someone who
doesn't want help. I absolutely wanted help and this
counselor slowly helped me – forced me – to open my eyes.

Sometimes he had me face things I didn't want to face. A good counselor does that.

It seemed important to specifically identify my own errors. If I did not do this, I would likely repeat them, with similar – or worse – results. That alone was enough to make me very, very motivated. I didn't know how I would ever survive going through this again.

For sure, I had been pretty active in submitting to George. Honestly, I didn't know what a truly Christian marriage looked like with submission held in a healthy balance. I had a lot to learn.

Practically speaking, on a day-to-day basis, my submission looked like me being a doormat. This dynamic of my marriage was identified early on by the counselor. After observing the two of us for two or three weeks, the counselor said he had observed enough to know one of the major dynamics of our marriage. What he said shocked me.

"Whenever there is a major decision to be made between the two of you," he turned to point at George, " he *always* wins. Always. Cindy, you *never* win."

I was completely shocked. He said it so clearly, so plainly. But if this was true, how could I have missed it? George, of course, did not like this, and promptly objected, saying it wasn't true at all.

The counselor told him that was the homework assignment. We had one week to come up with a single instance when he had yielded to me. And then these words. "I don't think you'll find one."

If this was true, then I had made a whole lot of mistakes. To allow such a pattern to control the marriage could never serve to make any marriage flourish. The sobering truth I had to face was that this did not happen without my active participation and agreement. This mistake went on my list.

And then there was the way I finally just stopped trying. Eventually I was so worn down that I lost hope and just settled into a new pattern. One day, I made a deliberate, conscious decision. I just stopped trying to reach out for a connection. I told myself I could do this. That was not true.

If I'm ever going to get healthy, I've got to tell myself the truth.

Part of that decision came from my attempt to put into practice what I had read in James Dobson's book, *Love Must Be Tough*. Changing my position from one of tugging on George's shirt sleeves like a small child trying to get his attention… to one of turning around and taking steps away from him was supposed to make him notice the new distance between us. Theoretically, he would miss the closeness, making him actually initiate movement toward me.

But that never happened. Instead, it seemed to calm me. It did create a new sense of peace, even if it was a peace built on an unsustainable platform. I just stopped trying to create closeness in any way. In the end, it only confirmed that he really wasn't interested in me at all.

At least if he couldn't maintain complete control. And that was not going to happen. Never again. I couldn't do it. Even if I wanted to, I couldn't do it.

Control was clearly one of the main issues. Even though it took me so many years to see this. I'm not sure how long it would have taken me, if I hadn't had a marriage counselor force me to see it.

As George began to sense that things were shifting, he reverted to passive-aggressive behavior. Sometimes passive-aggressive behavior can be worse than direct, open aggression. Because it's passive, it may not be easily detected. That can make it harder to identify and harder to figure out how to respond.

One example was how George insisted that I could not use rock salt to melt the ice on the concrete steps outside the door. With a malfunctioning leaky gutter directly over the steps dropping water onto each step, freezing winter temperatures quickly created a thick block of ice on the steps. The final straw was when the single hand rail broke off, making it truly treacherous to get down the five or six steps onto ground.

I asked if he could repair the hand rail and/or allow the use of rock salt, but once he knew this was something that mattered to me, George just refused to do either. He insisted that the salt was "hard on the concrete." Never mind that the slippery ice was hard on me!

It seemed like a clear demonstration as to what was important to him. Concrete steps? Or avoiding broken bones? Forget the words. The answer is clearly apparent by behavior. The kids seemed more agile and managed it okay, but I have always been unsure on slippery places and have fallen plenty of times.

This did not get fixed until I brought it up during a counseling session. Apparently feeling embarrassed was what it took. The railing was fixed within a week.

And using rock salt? I really need to own that one. That one's on me. Why didn't I just get some salt and use it when needed? That's what I wish I had done.

But I had never learned to think independently. From my earliest childhood, I had learned to fear my father. It was only a short leap to transferring that fear to my husband. Honestly, it did not occur to me to act in defiance of George's order. Today, that would never happen.

Another example of George's passive-aggressive behavior was about his complete disregard for my housekeeping. As a stay-at-home mom, I managed all the basic housekeeping. In addition to his full time job as a Chaplain, George enjoyed farming on the side, a hobby he relished. Through the years, the farming had grown from corn, strawberries, tomatoes, and other fruits and vegetables, to raising pigs, rabbits, ducks, and turkeys.

The pigs were the main farm animals. They acted like… well, pigs! They loved to roll in the mud. The mud, of course, was part earthen mess, and part manure. All mixed together.

When George tended to the pigs, he wore his farm boots as he trudged through the wet mess. The problem I had was about what he did when he needed to come inside for a bathroom break. The only bathroom in this old pre-civil war house was straight through the kitchen.

He used to take his dirty farm boots off, leaving them on the porch outside the door. That was a workable solution. But as the marriage continued its downward trajectory, a new passive-aggressive habit began.

George just trudged right through the kitchen, tracking that awful "mud" onto the clean linoleum floor. Apparently, I was supposed to follow behind him to clean it up. If I didn't, it would end up being picked up on everyone's shoes and carried throughout the house.

Sadly, yes – I did that. I cleaned it up. For a while. Until I finally just got tired of being treated this way. It sort of felt like a slap in the face to me. He tracked the mud-manure into the house. I was expected to clean it up.

So, I reminded him that he needed to remove his boots before stepping in to the house.

But my words didn't matter. Not at all. Finally I told him that if he wanted to track mud and manure in on the kitchen floor, he could clean it up himself.

Except… he didn't. In the end, he really didn't care.

I don't even want to think about this anymore. Just, it was awful.

Before, during, and after the separation, I was working full time for the local Pennsylvania State Representative. I filled the role of chief-of-staff and managed the three district offices. I began this job on Day #1 for the newly elected Representative.

Working closely with him worked well for the first two or three years. He liked having me write for him. He did have professional writers available to him from Harrisburg, but many times he just gave writing assignments to me. I drafted letters and news releases for him.

But the position and power seemed to change him in negative ways. ("Power corrupts. Absolute power corrupts absolutely."[3]) I tried to stay clear of all that, but sometimes it was just not possible.

The Representative knew who I was. After all, it was a small, rural community. Everyone sort of knew everyone else. And with a few years of working closely, he knew the value I placed on personal integrity.

One day the Representative realized that he had made a mistake. We all make mistakes! The question was, what do you do when you realize the mistake? The House of Representatives had pulled one of their infamous "all nighters" to force through some bills. Sort of like, just vote, and then we'll let you go home.

It was a recipe for mistakes. Of course some (or many) Representatives cast votes they had not had time to review adequately or confer with colleagues to review the pros and cons before voting.

When one of those middle-of-the-night votes made the local newspaper, angry constituents called to complain.

My boss's way of dealing with this unpleasantness was to call an all-staff meeting. All four of us in the main district office assembled in front of him to hear him explain what had happened.

---

[3] Attributed to Lord Acton

And then he said these words: "Somebody is going to have to lie for me." He did not intend to own up to any responsibility himself. The only question was, which one of us will have to lie for him.

That was a bit shocking. But as he looked around the room at the four of us, he stopped when he looked at me. "Cindy, you can leave the room."

He knew I would not lie for him. I just wouldn't. He knew me well enough by then to know the "liar" would not be me.

I gladly left, and a staff member was chosen and instructed on the "necessary" lie.

It was another experience that reminded me how important my personal reputation was. It was something I valued a lot. I wanted people to know that my words meant something. That to the best of my ability, my words will be truth.

Of course, there were times I missed it. Sometimes inadvertently. Still, even then, I knew what I had to do. Face it, apologize – first to God, then also to whomever knew about it.

Confession is good for the soul.

> *See God's hand in this? He affirmed my personal reputation for integrity, even in a tense job situation.*

He provided a counselor and funds to pay for the counseling.

CHAPTER 15

One of the really, really tough things I had to face during this season was navigating the hard conversations I had to have with each of my three kids.

Initially, I had to tell them I was moving out. George was not willing to even discuss it, let alone negotiate how to proceed with a separation that would minimize trauma for the kids. My counselor offered to assist me, and I relied on his professional guidance.

Later, when the "new normal" settled in with the separation, I had another conversation with each of the kids. The message I told them as clearly as I could was that I was working on my own emotional stability, with the professional help of a counselor, with the goal of seeing if the marriage could be restored. That was my goal.

I had ZERO intention of ever getting married again, so it was not hard for me to tell the kids this: I intended to remain married, even if I had to live apart. This had nothing to do with divorce. If God could do a miracle and put this marriage back together, that's what I wanted. That was my one goal. So what if it took 25 years? Or longer? I was okay with that.

I knew I needed the separation. Divorce? Nope. Didn't need it. Didn't want it. What would be the point? With no intention of ever getting married again, separation could go on the rest of my life.

This is how I explained it to the kids: even if it takes 25 years, that's okay. I would live my life single, and if I needed to give God 25 years to do what would surely take a miracle, that was okay with me. I would live my life separated and ready. Nothing is too hard for God, right?

At that time, no divorce papers had been filed. I didn't need it. In my mind, divorce would only be necessary if one of us wanted to remarry someone else. And I was sure of this: that would not be me.

> *God walked with me during some really tough conversations with my kids.*
>
> *Even after the many years of trauma, He held me faithful to the vows I'd made to marriage.*

Two things helped me make the awful decision to move out of the family home.

(1) It had become clear to me that there was a very real possibility that George might have me involuntarily committed to a psychiatric facility. He had hinted about this possibility.

(2) With that awareness, I realized that I would be leaving the home, one way or another.

This was an awful thought. *Involuntarily committed?* I knew George well enough by that time to take this seriously.

So I had a choice: Walk out the door while I could still leave on my own two feet, or wait to be carried out on a stretcher. Either way, my kids would lose having their mom in the home. It was a truly awful choice.

Years later, as I reflected back on this time, I also realized that God knew that when I am finally face-to-face with Jesus, I really want to be able to tell Him I had done everything I knew to do.

I am aware that each of us will face God and give an account of the life we lived. "So then, each of us will give an account of ourselves to God" (Romans 14:12). I know now that with a clear conscience, I can tell God I did my best.

As I look back on this whole season, I learned to recognize and identify key areas that, if different, might have produced better outcomes. One was the lack of support I received from my local church.

After serving faithfully in various church positions for ten years, my personal reputation was solid. I don't think anyone questioned my character or spiritual integrity.

I've already described my involvement in the local pro-life organization. My public reputation was solid.

And yet, at the absolute lowest point in my life, having moved out of the family home, it became clear that I would receive no support at all from my church.

In fact, in what felt like a slap in the face to me, just one week after the separation, George was allowed to fill the pulpit and preach in our local church.

That was a huge shock to me. But even through the ensuing months, not one person from church ever asked me to tell my side of the story.

From the safety of today, looking back on this, I can say unequivocally that this was a major mistake. First of all, George should never have been allowed to preach so soon after the separation. Second, someone from the church leadership (probably including the senior pastor) should have asked me to come in and explain what had happened and what my plans were. How could anyone know the real story if only one party was allowed to speak? That just seems obvious at face value.

Until both sides have been heard, who can even come to a conclusion?

Even assuming for a moment that the whole thing was due to sin on my part, where is the church's obligation to pray for me? And counsel me toward reconciliation?

None of that happened.

Who knows what might have happened if church leadership had followed a simple process to hear from both parties.

It still makes me sad.

CHAPTER 16

It was never just about me. Just as it was never only about George. It takes two to marry, but as I was learning, it only takes one to break it apart.

My new-found emotional stability was a welcome relief for me. But it wasn't going to last. At some point, George began to pressure me again. With my emotional wounds still fairly fresh, it wasn't hard for him to put me right back into the trauma/panic zone.

What triggered me? It was when George and I had to figure out various issues regarding the kids. As long as they were minors, there would be issues we had to deal with.

I think he knew the triggers. He called me one day about making decisions for one of the kids. I don't even remember who or what it was about. I managed to finish the conversation and hang up the phone.

And then again… all over again… I started to lose it. It was a Saturday, and I was home alone; my daughter had gone for a day with friends.

My panic zone began a rapid spiral downward. I knew instantly I was in serious trouble. Thankful that by now I had a few girlfriends who knew about my situation, I grabbed the phone. Quickly before I totally lost it, I called one friend to see if she was available to come and sit with me. She was not. So I thanked her and dialed again, asking another friend if she could come, and she said yes. She was willing and available to drop everything and come to my house.

> *Having girlfriends I could call was another way God provided care for me.*

What a lifesaver. I didn't need advice. I didn't need anyone to "fix" it. I just needed someone to be with me.

As soon as I hung up the phone, my panic let lose. I sobbed deeper sobs than I knew were even possible. I stood and paced back and forth in my tiny living room.

I could not stop.

My friend arrived and sat with me. Just gentle pats on my shoulder, soft strokes on my back. She offered no advice; she didn't need to. Not today.

I cried so much, for so long, eventually I lost my voice. I remember croaking out the words, *"What does he want from me?"* Over and over. Again and again.

What does he want from me?

Hours later, hoarse from the sobbing, I made a decision. I was desperate to make this all stop. Even though this made no sense to me, still it was the only concrete thing I could think of to do.

That was the day I made a decision.

Monday morning, I was going to call my attorney and instruct him to file divorce papers.

Why? I don't know. It was the only thing I could think of to do.

So that's what happened. The divorce papers were drawn up and served. But in my mind, I remained as clear as before. This had nothing to do with me wanting to be free to marry someone else. I was still ready to give God all the time He needed. Twenty-five years even. Or more. Wouldn't that be a wonderful testimony to the power of God?

So, my position didn't change. This was just a legal thing. Marriage was awful. At least for me. I felt like a complete and utter failure at being a good wife. So marriage for me was out of the question. That seemed obvious.

In the state of Pennsylvania, under no-fault divorce law, one only needs to allow two full years to pass, and it's done. I wasn't in any hurry. It didn't matter to me.

To my shock, once the divorce papers were served, the emotional abuse… stopped.

Things returned to reasonable calm. My emotional stability was back on track. I knew it would take time, but time was what I had. Twenty-five years, remember?

And then a month or two before it was due to be final, I heard from my attorney. George wondered if I would sign on the dotted line, making the divorce final… right then. No waiting for another month or two.

What? That made no sense to me. It was obvious something was going on, but I had no idea what. Do nothing, and it will be final very soon. It was sort of like he was initiating the divorce, only on his terms. What was the rush all of a sudden? Maybe it was just about control.

I signed. It was done. Whatever…

And then this: George was married very shortly after that. I forget exactly, but it was something like three months later.

It was so shockingly soon, even the kids were appalled. Had he been dating while still married? I have no idea. Whether he was dating while married or if it was just a super fast courtship, either was shocking.

See God's hand in this? He brought me a girlfriend to stay with me when I was in the midst of one of my darkest days.

Even though I could not see into the future, God held me to the marriage vow I had made.

Without any idea why, He did allow a new season of relative calm.

CHAPTER 17

Three years after the separation and subsequent divorce, I moved to Rochester, New York to be near family. My daughter was living with me at the time, and this move also gave her an opportunity for a fresh start. She agreed. She needed it. Both sons were in college, so my daughter was the only minor.

It was wonderful to turn a corner. It had become increasingly obvious that my five-year employment working for the State Representative was not going to last. He and I were seriously on different trajectories. The staff could not pretend we didn't see the numerous visits from a beautiful woman who came frequently and always closed the door to the private office. Yes, the Representative was married. The repeated visits from this woman seemed to be another secret we were supposed to keep.

But this was a small town, where "everyone knew everyone else," especially for elected officials and staff. I was so uncomfortable with people assuming that if I was working for him, he must be okay, based on my own reputation. As long as I worked for him, I provided him with cover. My own integrity cover. That made me very uncomfortable.

So the move to Rochester was good for me as well. I did it without a job lined up and with very little cash on hand. But I soon found work at a law firm, making enough money for rent and basic needs. Creating geographic space between me and George helped. No more risk of running into him at the grocery store or around town.

Living in Rochester, I loved the new calm. It gave me time to catch my breath. I joined a church and fully drank in great musical worship. It made my soul soar.

My daughter did well for most of the year. But something changed near the end of the school year. She made a sharp, sudden turn back into darkness. It sent me into panic again.

How does one parent a teen intent on breaking rules and laws? I was on my own here. Single parenting was never God's plan. I reached out to my church to request backup. They gave wonderful supportive help through their "Stephens Ministry" program. It was a compassionate one-on-one program, assigning trained volunteers to walk through a season of crisis with people in need.

I needed it! Many days, the weekly one-on-one meeting was a lifeline for me. This was a season for me to be on the receiving end of ministry. I also signed up to go through the church's Divorce Recovery program, another healing program.

> *Receiving this help from my church was another lifeline from God. I fully embraced the help from both programs.*

At the end of the year, after several personal and intense conflicts, my daughter moved back to live with her dad.

For the first time, I was really on my own.

CHAPTER 18

Slowly, I was healing. Slowly, tentatively, I began a little dating. It was so foreign for me to figure out how the "rules" had changed since I had last dated – decades ago! It sort of felt good. I really was healing. And with the remarriage of my ex, there was no longer the possibility of reconciliation and/or remarriage to him.

As I ventured out into the strange new world of single adults, a couple of things really shocked me. It seemed that a lot had changed.

My first shock was to adjust to a new self image. My previous dating experiences were largely when I was known as the sister of "the beauty queen." She was absolutely the beautiful one, the Homecoming Queen even. I never ever considered myself beautiful, or anything close. With frizzy, curly red hair and big, clunky glasses, wearing mostly hand-me-downs and having no real fashion sense, I just was who I was. Long ago, I had made peace with it. It was really okay with me.

But now, as a single in my late forties, it seemed that men found me attractive, something I had a hard time figuring out. It didn't make sense to me. The mirror doesn't lie. I was "plain Jane" through and through.

I mean, yes – my glasses had been replaced by contact lenses long ago, and my unruly red hair had finally been tamed with the aid of flat irons. I learned to apply just a bit of makeup, and I tried to find clothes with some style. None of this was in my strong suit.

When I first moved to Rochester, my sister and I rented an apartment together. One Saturday, she invited me to go with her to a dance, and it was sort of fun. I used to really love dancing way back when I was in high school.

That first time out, I did get asked to dance by several different men, but especially by a good-looking guy named Phillip.[4] He really was quite good-looking, so I was pretty sure he wasn't really interested in me. I know how it goes. And it's okay.

I totally thought he was using me as a way to get closer to my beautiful sister. That's how it had always worked in my world.

---

[4] Name changed

Turned out, he really was interested in me. And we dated for a few months. He was kind and a complete gentleman. I gently explored where he was in his faith journey, and learned that Christian faith was not something we shared. Nor was he interested. His ex-wife said she was a Christian, but nothing about her made him interested in Jesus… at all. Just the opposite, sadly.

That relationship ended peacefully and I returned to the singles dances, loving the movement and fairly safe environment. It's hard to explain how difficult it was to change my own self-perception. I was in my middle adult years. That's a lot of decades for me to "know" that my appearance was ordinary. Plain Jane me! How was I to make the shift to accept the fact that men looked at me differently? It was hard for me.

The other thing that totally shocked me was this. Eventually discovering online dating allowed me to meet some Christian men. At first I took it for granted that Christian men would understand and respect basic boundaries on physical contact.

That assumption turned out to be wrong. This wasn't exactly expected conversation for a first date, but sadly, I learned not to take this boundary for granted. So if we got past the first few getting-to-know-each-other dates, I learned that I had to give my little physical boundaries speech. I called it "The Talk."

It seemed to me like a natural assumption. It is one of the clear teachings from the Bible. Sex is reserved for a man and woman committed by marriage for life. So if I met a "Christian" guy, why wouldn't it make sense that he would share this value? Sadly, that just was not true.

How basic is this? To this day, I don't know what to make of it. It is possible some of these men were not truly Christians. Of course, it was not possible for me to know that.

Eventually, I ended up saying something like this: "I don't care if I'm the last person on the earth with this boundary. It's still my boundary. That's not going to change. If that's a problem for you, then just move on."

See God's hand in this? He held me steady in my personal commitment to physical boundaries. Even when I began to notice that some men found me attractive, I didn't change my position. And I never changed my internal dialogue: I just was who I was.

CHAPTER 19

In 1999, I enrolled in a twelve-month, degree-completion program at Roberts Wesleyan College. For a full year, I attended a four-hour class every Monday evening while continuing my full-time job working at a law firm. It was an intense year with a lot of reading and writing assignments. Almost all of our grades came from those writing assignments, which is where I flourish. I finished this program with a 4.0 GPA.

In May of 2000, I proudly walked across the platform to receive my Bachelor of Science degree. It was a goal that had been put on hold for so many years. It meant I changed the family legacy from at best finishing high school to… college? Sure! Absolutely! We were all capable of earning a college degree, all six of us siblings. I loved achieving this long-held goal.

Of course my own children and nieces and nephews went to college, but for my own generation, this was ground breaking.

After several years working hard to heal from my own emotional injuries, I actually felt like I might be open to the possibility of marriage. Spending those years working on my own issues turned out to be time well spent.

Exploring the world of online dating, I learned to be cautious. It was a fairly new thing back then. I decided to use a Christian site and eventually met someone who seemed like a possible husband.

All three of my kids were grown and gone. They were all scattered throughout Pennsylvania and New York state. I didn't see them very often, so eventually I decided that if I ever did meet someone online who seemed like a possible future husband, I would consider relocating. I limited myself to interactions with men who lived up and down the east coast. If I ever did meet someone and eventually marry, I wanted to make it simple to travel back and forth for visits with kids and for kids to visit me.

In the fall of 2001, I moved to central Florida to be near this Christian man I had met online. He had flown to Rochester to meet me in person, and I had flown to Orlando to meet his family and friends. After a few visits and lots of emails and phone conversations, it looked like there might be a promising future for us, so the next logical step was for us to live in the same town and just date. He still had a minor child at home, so I agreed to move.

He helped me find an apartment and a job. All seemed to be on a happy course for several months. Maybe there would be a happily-ever-after for me.

In due time, we did become engaged and were happily making wedding plans when I unexpectedly crashed and burned.

Out of the blue, I began having panic attacks. Each one was scary enough to make me ready to do just about anything to avoid another one. It began to feel like I was having "husband triggers."

Finally, I made the sad, painful decision to end the engagement. Gave back the ring, cancelled wedding plans, and tried to figure out what to do next.

To this day, I still think those awful, terrible, painful panic attacks were God's way of protecting me from what I eventually realized would have been a marriage deeply entrenched in codependency. So I gave thanks to God and moved on.

The panic attacks sent me searching for a counselor, who was the first to diagnose me with PTSD (Post Traumatic Stress Disorder). Apparently, the trauma I experienced through the prolonged time in my first marriage was enough to trigger me into panic attacks.

> *When I began to date, God held me steady in basic boundaries. He led me to enroll in a college program, earning my bachelor's degree. He nudged me to end an engagement, even though it was painful.*

CHAPTER 20

It was time for me to dig a little deeper into my own issue of codependency. Painful, but better than the alternative. *Thank You, God.*

I was now living in central Florida, and the only friends I had were "his" friends. But I realized I had really fallen in love with the Sunshine State and had no desire at all to move back into a snowy, cold climate. I did not see that coming.

Slowly I made my own friends from church. I made coffee dates with women where it was safe to share painful histories and joyful events. Girlfriends were important.

And then I decided to explore the world of ballroom dancing, something I had just begun to dabble in while still living in Rochester. I totally loved swing dancing and thought it would be good exercise plus a place to make new friends.

Turns out the ballroom dance community is a pretty safe place to meet and make new friends. The same general group of people shows up at the various ballroom dances around town. So I began to learn the basic ballroom dances (waltz, fox trot, swing, hustle, cha-cha, rumba, salsa, etc.). Once I learned the basic steps for these dances, I could follow anyone who asked me to dance. It was really fun. I invited some of my girlfriends from church to come. A few did.

Discovering the world of ballroom dancing was better than I expected. It was a social event as well as physical exercise. I really did love the movement of ballroom dancing. My favorite dance was the waltz. And it felt safe to me because even the physical touching is light and safe.

And that is how I met Charlie[5]. We seemed to have a lot in common, and he seemed to love worshipping God with me at my church. He liked planning romantic dinners; I liked being romanced. We did a lot of ballroom dancing.

A year later, we were engaged and began the three-month marriage prep course at my church. Four months after that we were married.

I did not have panic attacks. Not even one. I interpreted this to be God's blessing on the marriage. After

---

[5] Name changed

one painful, broken engagement, I had created a new rule for myself. I would not even consider engagement until I knew someone at least a full year. That rule was my way of protecting myself. It made me feel safer.

Sadly, shockingly, it began to fall apart just days after the wedding. On our honeymoon, he seemed to change into a very scary person. With no visible triggers that I could see, he would explode into rage. It scared me. I have never done well with scary out-of-control yelling or any displays of strong anger. During these episodes, even his language switched into awful profanity. During the coming months, he began to leave for three or four days at a time.

By this time, I had learned some life-changing lessons from the counseling I had been through and from reading the *Boundaries* book so many times. My daily Bible reading was still a strong foundation.

I reviewed: boundaries are never about the "other" person. Boundaries are for me. I decide what is acceptable and what is not. And then, it is up to me to enforce my boundaries.

I was a little slow to implement this, but once I realized that this was not just someone having a bad day – that it was an ongoing issue – I was ready. The next time Charlie flew into a rage, profanity spewing, I calmly looked at him and said, "When you act like that, it is a clue to me that you are out of control. When you are calm again, I am glad to talk about any issues you want to discuss." And after saying that, I turned and walked out of the room. Leaving him alone in a room stopped the verbal attack in its tracks. Apparently, it's no fun ranting and raving in an empty room.

God was definitely using the boundaries lessons to help me. Where did I get the strength to confront this new abuse? God. He walked with me.

Treat me well, or not at all. Yes. That.

I did that a few times. Always calmly, always leaving him alone in the room. My new counselor advised me to pack an overnight bag to leave in the trunk of my car... just in case. If going into another room was ever not enough, or if I ever felt physically threatened, I could jump into my car and drive away.

I did that. I began to feel like I could take care of myself. My overnight bag included supplies of prescriptions needed, important papers, and a few clothes. It was also important to have some people in my corner. Not wanting to make the same mistakes again, I did confide in my sisters and a few girlfriends.

Having friends to confide in was enormously important and helpful. God

was nudging me and the assurance of
His presence made me feel stronger.

Charlie never struck me physically, but seeing him act out his rage on objects was scary. Was it only a matter of time before he escalated to striking me? The day he stormed out of the house and picked up a ladder in the garage only to SLAM it down was a clue. He seemed to need something physical to act out.

Eventually, he asked if I would oppose him if he filed divorce papers; I said no and agreed to a simple divorce. It meant I had to walk through what seemed to be my worst possible nightmare.

Me… divorced? *Twice?* How is that possible? I hold marriage in very high regard. I believe God intended marriage to be "one man, one woman, for life."

It was an awful season for me. Slowly I began putting the pieces together. I thought he just enjoyed a glass of wine with dinner. Coming from a completely teetotaler tradition, having an occasional glass of wine with dinner actually seemed to reassure me that this wouldn't be a rigid, legalistic thing. In an odd twist, it made me feel more secure.

To join him, I would also order a glass of wine with dinner, but I only drank half; he drank the rest of my wine.

Turns out he was a closet alcoholic. I had no idea. As I struggled to figure it out, I began to wonder about the wine. We went to a marriage counselor once. I raised the issue then. Hearing the "a" word (alcohol) made Charlie really angry at me. After leaving the counselor, Charlie spit out these words: "Would it make you happy if I stopped drinking for a week?" YES... And then I heard these shocking words: "Well then, I might as well stop the pills too."

Pills? *What pills?* The next time he left the house, I went to his medicine cabinet to discover... opiods. I had no idea. Eventually, I realized he was also addicted to gambling.

With no real experience with addictions, I sought a counselor who specialized in addiction recovery. My codependency was my issue. Again.

Sigh

It was back to counseling for me.

I found a wonderful, compassionate, Christian counselor who had gone through her own addiction and recovery with her husband. She taught me a lot, and referred me to a weekly 12-step recovery program where people listened to a recovering addict talk during the first hour and we then spent the second hour in our assigned small group of people with similar addictions. I was assigned to a group of women working on recovering from codependency. Boy, did I ever have a lot to learn.

Notice how God directed me. I found a counselor who specialized in addiction recovery. That was hugely important to me. My own addiction of codependency was something I had to learn to identify and recover from.

People sometimes say "once an alcoholic, always an alcoholic." In fact in the 12-step recovery meetings for alcoholics, they always start out by going around the room, introducing themselves: "Hi; I'm Cindy (insert your own name), and I'm an alcoholic."

For me, this meant "Hi; I'm Cindy, and I'm a codependent." Codependent in recovery, but still... If I don't "own" it, I will be prone to fall back into addiction.

By this time, I just decided I was really done with marriage. Two failed marriages? It was better—*by far*—to be single and lonely than to be married and in crisis. I was really done. By this time, I had some girlfriends and a few guy friends. My co-facilitators from Divorce Recovery were also wonderful friends.

That second marriage didn't even make it to a full year. The end of this marriage put me into a season of grieving and soul-searching. I needed it.

I had to learn to say the words: *I have been married and divorced twice*. It was really hard for me to say it. Without choking. And yet, it was the truth.

I was embarrassed. I was in pain.

I have been married and divorced twice.

It helped that the marriage lasted such a short time. I knew him for a year before the engagement and the marriage ended after eleven months. My grief was absolutely intense, but it didn't last nearly as long as my grief following my first divorce. In leading groups through Divorce Recovery, I had learned that it takes about a year's recovery for every five years of marriage.

That had been true for me. After my 22-year marriage ended, I needed five years to process my grief and learn new lessons. But although this second marriage of less than one year plunged me into intense grief, the grief was fairly short lived.

In two months, I knew I still needed some social outlet, and I was ready to head back out to ballroom dancing.

> *See God's hand in this? He walked with me through this very dark period. He provided a wonderful, warm Christian counselor with a specialty in addictions. He led me into a small group for weekly Bible study and prayer.*

CHAPTER 21

And that is exactly how I first met Mickey![6] January 8, 2005, Mickey and I both showed up at the same ballroom dance. We spotted each other from across the room. We both liked what we saw. I did not recognize him, although I realized later that I had seen his ex-wife a few times at dances.

He thought I was cute, and I thought he was handsome. Tall, dark, and handsome. With my intention to remain single, I knew from the start that this was safe for me. I "knew" no romantic relationship would come from this. Why? Because during our very first dance together, the conversation included mention of his two sons' Bar Mitzvahs.

---

[6] Name not changed!

So there were three reasons I felt safe. Mickey was: (1) too tall for me, (2) too young for me – appearing about a decade younger than I, and (3) too Jewish for me.

Too tall. Too young. Too Jewish.

He can be a friend!

He would never be a potential marriage partner, so let's just get to know each other and have fun. And who knows? Maybe God can use me in his life.

At first, that seemed to be what Mickey was doing also. He was exploring the new world of being single in his forties (I was mid-fifties). I saw him dance with lots of different women. He was not zeroing in on any one. Perfect. It actually made me feel safer with him. He was clearly not pursuing me or any other woman. As I learned later, he was also badly scarred from his own 22-year marriage, so not looking for a potential marriage.

> *God really did have a plan for us, but He knew that we had to go slow.*

With the passage of time, as we got to know each other, we did begin casual dating. I knew – because he told me – that he was dating several different women. This was so perfect! It totally worked for me. In actuality, it served to lower my guard. Eventually, his other dates dwindled down one by one, until it was… only me.

But we were both pretty badly bruised from our marriage history, so there was no pressure at all from either of us. We just enjoyed getting to know each other. We told each other our stories, and it felt good to get it out. There was validation going both directions. I knew he was good for me, and I think I was good for him.

Eventually, Mickey invited me to join him for his Sunday morning church, which turned out to be a Unity Church. I said sure!

This raises an obvious question. How is it that a Jewish man goes to… a church?

Turns out, some time ago he and his then-wife began attending the Unity Church as part of spiritual exploration. Unity churches tend to be fairly involved in addiction recovery, which was good. Unity churches like to "do good" deeds. There is no mention of salvation, repentance, or conversion.

So I went to a Sunday morning Unity Church service with Mickey and a week later, I invited him to join me at my church. He loved my church, and after just one visit, he never left. That meant he was hearing sermons and worship music every single week. He had lots of questions, and I did my best to answer them.

I was aware of the Bible's warning that Christians should not date an unbeliever. Having been in a 22-year marriage that felt like being "unequally yoked," I wholeheartedly agree. Don't get into a long-term relationship with someone not committed to Jesus!

Two things made this different. First, it became clear early on that God was doing something here, and I had a front row seat to watch what He was doing!

And second, from the start, I absolutely intended to remain friends. Casual hanging out. Mickey was openly dating several women.

And yet, as Mickey and I continued just hanging out together, I realized that even though this wasn't even close to a possible marriage track, still he was not a Christian, so why would I expect him to behave like one? It was time for... The Talk.

By now, I had a brief script I'd used before. *I don't care if I'm the last person on the earth with this boundary. It's still my boundary. That's not going to change. If that's a problem for you, then just move on.* Yeah, that script.

I actually thought that would be the end of Mickey. Why wouldn't it be?

But it wasn't! God really did have a plan going on here. Mickey stuck around. He has since told me that he was pretty fascinated and curious about what made me so different. Turns out that what made me different was... Jesus!

I was also continuing the weekly Home Group meetings I had been in for Bible study and prayer. Eventually, I invited Mickey to come. He had so many questions, especially after each church service. Let him ask these people his never-ending questions!

It was a good move; he needed to get to know some godly men. Plus the Bible study was really helpful for Mickey to get to know this good Book.

> *God was clearly leading Mickey on a path that only led to… the cross.*

At some point, I told Mickey that a person is either "on the bus" or not. It was a metaphor I used to explain that until a person makes that personal decision to follow Jesus, they remain on the outside. To me, it looked like Mickey was running alongside the bus, enjoying the sights and sounds and people, but never getting ON the bus.

At the end of each weekly meeting of our Home Group, we'd go around the room so each person could request prayer for specific things. When it was Mickey's turn, he began to say, "Pray that I'll get on the bus." Every week, that's what he said.

And I would wonder: Why don't you just get on the bus already? I didn't get it. What was holding him back?

And yet, I knew God was in charge. God was clearly leading Mickey along, step by step.

> *God made sure Mickey and I were both at that fateful dance on that day.*
>
> *He kept me solid in my decision to never marry again.*
>
> *He drew Mickey into a church that worshiped the true God.*
>
> *He brought Mickey into a small group for Bible study.*

CHAPTER 22

And then there was that day… Sunday, March 12, 2006.

Mickey and I had been hanging out, getting to know each other for more than a full year. He was joining me for church services and weekly Home Group meetings for more Bible study and prayer.

He had been asking people to pray that he would "get on the bus" for some time.

And then, it was time.

I just love it when God gets to move things along according to His own timetable.

That Sunday, our pastor showed a brief excerpt from the movie, *Passion of the Christ*. It was close to Easter, and the movie excerpt helped people visualize the immense cost to Jesus when He went to the cross.

As we left church that morning, Mickey said, "Maybe that's what I need. I'm a visual person. Maybe I should see that movie."

That's all I needed to hear! I decided if that's what it's going to take, then we're going to see that movie *before the sun goes down.*

We found the movie, rented it, and settled in my living room to watch it. (There's a fascinating, almost funny story about our renting this movie. That story is written in our previous book, *Simply Trusting God.*) A few times I glanced at Mickey, wondering how he was doing as some graphic scenes came on the screen.

It didn't take long. Mickey is a very feeling sort of guy with a wonderful tender heart, and there was no doubt at all on this day. He had tears streaming down his face.

When the movie ended, I turned to Mickey and simply said, "Do you want to pray?" He said yes!

Mickey took the plunge. He closed his eyes and through tears, asked Jesus to forgive his sins! Mickey was ready to surrender his whole life to following his new Savior.

And from that moment on, his spiritual growth took off like a rocket.

And I was in for a surprise. That very week my heart took me completely by surprise. I had already grown to really love Mickey, but now that he was a Christian, my heart took a giant leap upward. His decision to follow Jesus meant there was nothing to stand in our way. We were now together serving God.

Be still, my beating heart!

> *There is so much to thank God for here. Mickey had followed God's nudging straight to the cross of Christ! And after that, his own faith really did grow by leaps and bounds.*

In the goodness of our great God, who alone knows all things, He knew Mickey needed time for his new faith to grow. It was important that enough time passed so anyone could see that Mickey's faith was the real deal. That's not something that can be known in a day, a week, or a month. It takes the passage of time to observe.

Was this just an act done to win me over? Or was Mickey's faith genuine? That's a question that can only be answered with the passage of time.

And sure enough, his faith only grew. Anyone who knew him could see that. And hear it. Mickey, the consummate extrovert, was very vocal about his decision to follow Jesus.

Easter was right around the corner. Mickey celebrated his first Easter with great joy! Every chance he got, he told people, "This is my first Easter!" To the person in line beside him at the post office. To the person at the grocery store. To strangers everywhere. It was such good news to him, there was no stopping him.

All of it thrilled me. As months went by, our love continued to grow. And by December, Mickey was ready to shop for a ring. I learned that Mickey can definitely keep a secret. I had no idea he was shopping for a diamond ring! He actually found the most perfect, beautiful diamond ring I have ever seen. And he never told me!

Next, he planned a perfect setting for his proposal. We met at a ballroom dance, so proposing marriage at a ballroom dance was so perfect.

We went to the Friday night dance, where he had arranged for the song "Could I Have This Dance For the Rest of My Life" to play, and then he got down on one knee. He pulled a ring box out of his pocket, opened it, looked up at my shocked face, and said those magic words. "Will you marry me?"

I said YES!

That began a wonderful whirlwind of activity as we set a date and began making wedding plans. We found a house to buy, closed on it a week after our wedding, and moved our two households into one. It was a magical, fabulous time for us.

Now, life really changed. For the first time in my life, I had a husband who was absolutely sold-out to Jesus! I had no idea, however, how much that alone would change my own life. This was really brand new territory for me.

Now 13 years married to Mickey, I can tell you this:

> *Without a doubt, being in a marriage with both partners totally committed to serving God is a completely different experience.*

I know because I've had it both ways. Trust me, it makes all the difference in the world when both partners are truly "all in" with their commitment to follow Jesus, no matter what.

Mickey and I read from the Bible together nearly every morning. We pray together every day. Usually twice a day.

And every day, if either one of us senses that something might be wrong, or just a little "off," we bring it up and talk it through. This marriage is a safe place.

Here's another thing that is true: I have grown more in my own faith during these thirteen years married to Mickey than at any other period in my entire life. Prior to Mickey, to a large extent, I was pretty much flying solo. I could do all the things I knew to do (spiritual disciplines of daily Bible reading, praying, attending church, participating in a small group, leading groups, etc.), and doing all those things did help my faith to continue growing.

But... do not miss this: being in a close, transparent relationship (married or otherwise) makes your own faith journey grow like nothing else. This was another unexpected bonus from God's own hand.

We learned that it was safe to say those magic words: *I am sorry. I was wrong. Please forgive me.*

Yes, those are magic words! I said them to Mickey, and Mickey said them to me. As often as needed.

It took me a few years, actually, to really believe in every cell of my being that Mickey not only loved me, but was completely committed to me, to this marriage. It turns out I was so habituated by feeling alone in life that although it was true in my head – I knew I was no longer alone – it was not yet in my heart. I had felt completely alone from my earliest memories as a young child. I was now in my mid-fifties.

What did it take for me to get it? Well, time is part of the answer. But the real reason I got it was because Mickey was so consistent, every time, across time. Day after day, year after year, he always made me feel safe. He had my back. On a good day. On a bad day. He was ready and available to defend me, take care of me (if/when needed), and just be there. It was truly amazing!

sigh

Yep, I love this guy!

And... Thank YOU, God!

'Cause, for sure, God did that!

> *See God's hand in this? He had a plan for Mickey's conversion, at just the right time. And after Mickey's conversion, God gave both of us patience for most of a year, while Mickey's faith grew. God flooded us with joy!*

CHAPTER 23

A significant thing happened to me around 2012.

I read Tim Keller's book *Counterfeit Gods*. It was truly eye-opening for me. In this book, Keller identifies some common false gods especially common in Americans, even if they are unknown to us. Or maybe not realized.

Keller's book has a diagnostic question for readers to answer; it's intended to help identify any counterfeit gods someone might have. By this time I had been seriously following Jesus for nearly 50 years. I didn't think I had any idols hidden away. Actually, I was pretty sure of it.

But Keller's diagnostic question made me rethink this whole thing. He asks this question:

What is it in my life that causes me (or has caused me) the most intense discomfort?

Answering that question honestly is a clue to what my hidden idols might be.

What is it, that if taken away from me, would send me into a tailspin?

When I consider that simple, direct question, the answer is immediately obvious to me. There is one thing that almost took me down.

Divorce.

If Keller's question is indeed the diagnostic question, then my counterfeit god is... being married.

> *God must have known that it would take a question this direct to make me face what had been a counterfeit god in my life. He used Keller's book to nudge me to face this truth.*

I had tried everything I knew to make marriage work. *Twice.* And that ended up in failure. *Twice.*

After my first marriage led to a separation, I still had a singular, clear intent: to help me recover enough emotional stability so I could get back to focusing on... *saving the marriage.*

I really had to ponder this. It was such a game-changer question for me. I thought about it a lot. Always leery of blind spots, I asked a few trusted friends what they thought.

It's sort of like this: How do you tell who the alcoholic is? You have a table full of adults gathering for dinner and a glass of wine. But then they learn no wine is available. Most of them shrug it off. No big deal. Except one person who seems really upset. He may even suggest leaving this restaurant and going somewhere else… where they have wine.

How do you tell who the alcoholic is? Take the alcohol away. That's how you know.

How do you know what the counterfeit god is? Take it away.

Keller reminds me that a counterfeit god is usually when a person takes something that is *truly good*, and makes it into something *ultimate*. Marriage fits the mold for me. For sure, marriage is something God made, and it was a good thing. Marriage is a *very* good thing. It just cannot be an *ultimate* thing.

I still think about it from time to time. Both of my divorces (especially the first one) were devastating to me. It wasn't even the loss of the husband that was so devastating. It was the divorce itself. The failure of my marriage.

Was it true that I "needed" to be married? That was the question I had to face.

I continued to ponder it. I prayed, asking God for insight. Eventually, I reluctantly concluded that yes – it was true for me. I had been carrying around a counterfeit god for decades.

After my second divorce, I really did make a decision: I was DONE with marriage. It was too painful for me. There was no way I was going to risk going through that again. I repeated my new mantra: *Better – by far – to be single and lonely that to be in a loveless marriage*. Both of my failed marriages evolved into more than just leaving me lonely. Both marriages were profoundly emotionally abusive.

I knew that God hates divorce; so did I. As I worked to process this new thought, I recognized that it had nothing to do with marriage itself being a good thing. A very good thing. It's just that marriage can never be an *ultimate* thing – a counterfeit god.

Maybe it's similar to what we read in Luke 14:26. "If anyone comes to me and does not hate father and mother, wife and children, brothers and sisters—yes, even their own life—such a person cannot be my disciple."

The CEV translation says it this way:

> "You cannot be my disciple, *unless you love me more than you love your father and mother, your wife and children, and your brothers and sisters*. You cannot come with me unless you love me more than you love your own life" (italics mine).

Of course we are to love our father and mother! And our spouse and children! Jesus is making the point that even that love cannot be higher than the way we love Him.

So, yes, I should absolutely hold marriage in high regard. *Just not higher than Jesus.*

Somehow, letting go of my grip on marriage seemed to be the key. I let it go. Completely.

It was wonderful. The only ONE thing I really needed was... a person: Jesus.

See God's hand in this? When the time was right, God brought Tim Keller's book into my life. The diagnostic question made it clear.

And then, God (the real God) helped me give up that long-held counterfeit god.

CHAPTER 24

But is it biblical?

It has been a long, painful journey to process my own two divorces. After all, I am a staunch believer in one marriage, for life. How do I make peace with myself? God hates divorce. So do I. It's time to address the question head-on: Was my divorce biblical? (I am referring here to my first divorce after a 22-year marriage. My second divorce was short and simple, and was initiated by my husband.)

Recently, I came across a book written by Gary Thomas titled *When to Walk Away: Finding Freedom From Toxic People*[7]. Gary is a well-known Christian former pastor, now a writer and speaker, with more than twenty books to his name. He brings insights from his many years serving as a pastor.

---

[7] Gary Thomas, *When to Walk Away*, Zondervan, Grand Rapids, Michigan, 2019.

One of the key points Gary makes is that there is a difference between "difficult" people and "toxic" people. It's an important distinction. If I'm married to a difficult person, that calls for one strategy. On the other hand, if it's a toxic person, that's a completely different scenario and calls for a very different plan.

If I am in a difficult marriage and intend to be faithful to my marriage vows, I need to marshall all the resources I can and get to work! There are many wonderful stories of difficult marriages that were fought for and eventually (after a lot of hard work) restored.

On the other hand, if it becomes increasingly obvious that I am dealing with much more than a difficult marriage – if, in consultation with an experienced Christian marriage counselor, it becomes obvious that I am in a toxic marriage, with a toxic partner, then that calls for a different strategy.

Gary points out that the initial issue to be dealt with is safety. I resonated with this. I needed the space of a separation so that I could recover from the many years of toxicity.

Throughout the book, Gary often substitutes the word "evil" for "toxic." With the first priority being safety, you may have to leave to protect your own safety, and the safety of any children in the home.

Probably the single strongest argument he makes for a spouse leaving is the surprisingly long list of times when

Jesus left people. He references various stories throughout the chapters, but helpfully, he includes an Appendix with seven pages of Bible verses and references showing Jesus walking away, leaving people behind.

Chapter 17 is devoted specifically to *toxic marriages*. "A *toxic* marriage isn't just frustrating; it's also *destructive*. It's marked by unrepentant, controlling behavior from which the spouse refused to repent" (p. 168, emphasis in original).

Gary goes on to say, "We live in a fallen world where some of the most beautiful things are turned into vehicles of ugly manipulation and abuse. Because some toxicity can reach such a high level, there are times in the name of confronting evil when *it is necessary for a spouse to act like Jesus and walk away* (emphasis added)" (p. 168).

Reading these words makes me feel validated. Allowing the situation to devolve to a point where if I didn't get out, I might be involuntarily committed to psychiatric care, seems clearly to reach this level. Allowing it to get that bad? That was something both of us had done. We had both allowed that. As I openly, honestly search my heart, I do believe Jesus sadly affirmed leaving my marriage was necessary.

Jesus once said, "*no one who has left home or wife* (emphasis added) or brothers or sisters or parents or children for the sake of the kingdom of God will fail to receive many times as much in this age, and in the age to come eternal life" (Luke 18:29-30). Don't miss this: Jesus acknowledged that there would be times for someone to *leave a spouse*.

On page 174, the book includes the following quote from M. Scott Peck. "Since the primary motive of the evil is disguise, one of the places evil people are most likely to be found is within the church. What better way to conceal one's evil from oneself, as well as from others, than to be a deacon or some other highly visible form of Christian within our culture."

Another really helpful idea from *When to Walk Away* is on page 175. Gary points out something that might seem obvious to readers, but applied to toxicity in marriage makes sense. God has very clear teaching about keeping the Sabbath. First found in the Old Testament, we read how serious it was to fail to keep this commandment. The penalty? Death! Numbers 15:32ff makes it shockingly clear.

And yet, didn't Jesus himself break the Sabbath sometimes? It angered the Pharisees and they always called him out on it. But Jesus pushed back, telling them, "The Sabbath was made for man, not man for the Sabbath" (Mark 2:27). This happened so many times; it seems God wanted people to know that *people were more valuable than rules*.

If this is true (and it's hard to argue otherwise), then applied to a toxic marriage it seems clear that of two bad options, it is better for a spouse to leave than stay and be destroyed.

People matter to Jesus more than marriage.

CHAPTER 25

Living life married with Mickey as my partner was such a major new experience. It is hard to overstate the difference it made in my life having a true spiritual partner. Early on we began the habit of reading the Bible together and praying together every morning. As we read, we talked about how this chapter or that verse spoke to me, or to him, and especially, if it showed changes we needed to make.

We confessed sin as soon as either of us became aware of it. We forgave each other. Marriage grew into a wonderful, blessed space. We laughed together. A lot.

None of that happens unless we both feel safe. And praying together? That's a very intimate and vulnerable thing to do. Praying itself requires one to shed any pretense at least if it's really, actually, truly prayer. Of course, we've all heard plenty of prayers that weren't really prayers at all. Public prayers are often turned into mini-sermons, aimed at an individual, or group of people. But the two of us coming together to the very throne of God? That is an incredible experience.

Along the way, we came up with a structure for the intercessory prayer that was so important to us. Every day we made room for worship and awe. We gave thanks for the ways we noticed God at work. And then we made a list for people and situations we wanted to pray for every single day. Then we made a Monday list, a Tuesday list, etc., where we would write down what we wanted to pray for once a week.

On the very top of the "every single day" list was family, especially those who aren't yet following Jesus. And for Christian family, we prayed for them too, including any specific things we knew about. Each name gets lifted up in prayer, one by one. Every day.

Sweet… Sometimes the air itself seemed sweet. This was holy ground.

God blessed that. Prayer became increasingly, especially important when we lived through seasons of shockingly tight budgets. Yes, plural. **Seasons. Budgets**.

Seasons when it appeared there was no way to keep the electric on, water on, food on the table, plus make a really large mortgage payment. But God's Word, along with the George Mueller story[8] we had so internalized, proved

---

[8] See *Simple Trust, Simple Prayers*, available on Amazon

sufficient. We loved Ephesians 3:20 and memorized it. God is "able to do immeasurably more than all we ask or imagine, according to his power that is at work within us."

That one verse brought joy to our hearts! And here's what is true: We never missed a single meal. We never missed paying a bill. We were never even late paying a bill.

> *God held us steady as we did our best to honor Him. We talked about trusting God; now it was time to live it out.*[9]

And after months and even years of this, we would look back and wonder at the goodness of God, who never runs out. It seemed that God was pleased to trust us to take on this journey of learning to trust Him more and more.

During the lean seasons, we continued our commitment to tithing. The first 10% always went to our local church. It was one tangible way we could demonstrate that we were really trusting God to provide for our needs.

And then we would have a season with finances flowing easily. Money flowed in sufficiently that we did not have to worry or even wonder how we would pay the bills. Yes, we enjoyed those seasons. Yes, it was nice. But even then, we

---

[9] See *Simply Trusting God*

reminded each other that this season might change. And it always did.

Somewhere along the way, the financial winds seemed to be one of the main tools God used to stretch us in our individual spiritual growth.

That and... my health.

> *See God's hand in this? He gently gave us time to learn what marriage is like when both partners' first priority is loving God and serving Him. He nudged us to confess sin any time it was needed. He helped us forgive each other.*
>
> *He led us through financial ups and downs, while we learned to trust Him in every season.*

CHAPTER 26

Health Issues

I suppose telling the story of my personal faith journey would not be complete without talking about my health. As far as I can remember, I have had this issue my whole life. It is my old familiar nemesis.

My diagnosis has several names. I usually call it what it was called way back when I first got the diagnosis: Chronic Fatigue Syndrome (CFS). More recently, it has been called ME/CFS (Myalgic Encephalomyelitis), or SEID (Systemic Exertion Intolerance Disease). It's sort of like having Mononucleosis, except it never goes away.

Generally, I have profound fatigue every hour of every day. That's my main symptom. The fatigue is so profound, it doesn't come close to the other symptoms that must also be managed: pain, and having a low-functioning immune system.

I generally don't talk about it much. I don't really even think about it much. I'm used to it. It's my life.

After many decades, I have learned that almost no one gets it. It is an invisible disease. I look fine.

If I do talk about it, people want to fix me. Nearly always. It gets old. No, it just isn't even remotely true that if I "just take a nap," or "just rest 10 or 15 minutes," (things I've heard my whole life), or maybe "try taking this vitamin" I'll feel fine.

No, no, and please NO! None of those even come close to touching it. How do I know that? Because I have tried nearly every one of them and more. So please... just stop.

The current literature says that one of the main characteristics that serves to differentiate it from other, similar disorders is that "symptoms get worse within 12 to 24 hours following physical, mental, or emotional exertion."[10]

That means I have to monitor and limit the amount of physical, mental, or emotional exertion needed in any given day. Or week.

As the years pass, the fatigue seems to be growing. For the last few years, I have rarely gone out at all during evening hours. Sometimes I try. And Mickey is amazing and awesome about taking it all in. By mid-afternoon, I begin a

---

[10] From nih.gov

descent into physical and mental low function. In a way, it's easy. Because it is so predictable, I just don't plan things for late afternoons or evenings. Nor do I make important decisions that I might regret by morning.

In addition, I have not slept in a bed for several years. Lying flat is really hard on my back, so I sleep in a recliner chair. That works.

But what is there to complain about? My physical limitations are just things to manage as best I can. There's nothing here to complain about. I remember these words, written by the apostle Paul:

> He said to me, "My grace is sufficient for you, for my power is made perfect in weakness (2 Corinthians 12:9)."

Yes, I have asked God for healing. Many, many times. So it seems that God has a better plan. Better than healing. When I pray, I always yield to God. If He knows something I don't know, how arrogant would I be to imply that what I want is the better plan?

I also have a heart condition that I must manage. First diagnosed in 1988 as mitral valve prolapse (MVP), it began sending my heart rhythm on speed races. Wearing a heart monitor for 24 hours revealed a heart rate that reached 220 beats per minute. The rapid heartbeat was labeled supraventricular tachycardia.

Initially I took meds to regulate my heart rhythm, but I stopped taking them just a few years later when I realized my heart was behaving itself.

Since that time, I have learned that my heart will absolutely take off on a speed race any time I experience emotional stress. Divorce #2 proved that without a doubt. So I consider it my responsibility to manage stressful events. I limit my exposure, and my heart thanks me. It's sort of my own early warning system. My body tells me the truth. Even when I am slow to admit that I'm feeling stressed.

It probably helps that I am completely prone to… not worry. I think I missed the "worry gene."

That's probably enough about that. ☺

CHAPTER 27

1968 – 2019: Financial Journey

This telling would not be complete without some reflection on the financial side of my life. In a recent conversation with Mickey, I realized how many times my personal finances have come right down to the bottom of the barrel. And yet the real story is how God always, always provided for me.

From my first move to Rochester in 1968 (after graduating from ECPI in Pittsburg), I had very little cash on hand. I don't recall any worry at all; I just knew I had to find a job – any job at first. That's what I did. Was it a great job? No. Did I love it? Absolutely not. But it was a job, and as long as I was taking a paycheck from an employer, I felt like I owed them the best work I could do. That work ethic helped me a lot.

I really have to mention this: By the time I landed in what was my first real church (Brighton Community Church), one of the treasured books I read from their library was *Answers to Prayer*[11]. It was the story of George Mueller, and reading it absolutely changed my life.

Many years later, with support and encouragement from my sweet husband Mickey, I even published a completely rewritten, updated version of Mueller's writings. *Simple Trust, Simple Prayers* was my first published book.

Mueller's entire life was built on a simple premise: that God could be trusted to provide for material needs. The stories he told were stunning, and yet – why? Why was it stunning? *Why isn't simply trusting God the norm for people who claim to trust God?*

Trusting God made sense to me back then. It still makes sense to me. For Mueller, it was not a passing stage of life. He kept detailed journals for more than eight decades.

Those lessons sank deep into my soul. Maybe it helped that I came to Jesus with a blank slate. I didn't have any family history that contradicted the simple life George Mueller showed me. It became my habit to simply trust God. If/when times became financially tight, I searched my heart

---

[11] Now paraphrased using modern English, published *as Simple Trust, Simple Prayers*. Available on Amazon.

to make sure there were no hidden, secret sins lurking about. If any were found, I knew what to do.

Confess, repent, and receive the fresh breeze of my forgiving God!

Confess, repent, repeat.

And always continue tithing. That's one way I can tangibly demonstrate that I really do trust God. And then… hang on! God will provide. And sure enough… He always has.

I have never missed a single meal. I have never not had a roof over my head. In fact, as I consider most people living on the earth, across centuries of time, I realize that I am still… one of the rich ones. Seriously, I am one of the richest people that ever lived! I am in the 1%.

There is only room for gratitude for my life.

Around the year 2000, I was living and working in Rochester. I was working at a small law firm, doing some paralegal work and managing the office. Not willing to engage in any level of flirting, dating, or otherwise personal relationship with the owner of the firm, I found myself in an increasingly uncomfortable situation. After working there for two years, there was finally the proverbial "straw that broke the camel's back." My annual performance review.

Apparently my lack of personal interest in dating the boss made him decide to blame me for some of his own shortcomings. He put it all in writing in my performance review. I felt excoriated. I sat numbly through it, went home, cried some tears, and then wrote my response. The next day, I arrived at work with my two-week notice to quit, along with my own perspective on the performance review, which I wanted placed in my personnel file.

Of course, I immediately began a search for new employment. I had no real nest egg to fall back on. My paychecks pretty much paid for rent and food, but there was never enough to build up a reserve fund. And I had recently completed my college degree, spending my last nickel to pay for that.

No new jobs opened up, and at the end of those two weeks, I turned in my keys and walked out the door.

What now, God?

I knew He knew. I just didn't know yet. It's always so fun to look backward at life. It seems easy to see God's fingerprints. But as you go forward through life? Not always easy.

And yet this was true. I seriously did not worry. I did, however, seriously search. And God honored that. Just in the nick of time… a new job.

Sometimes it's just FUN to see how God works. This was one of those times.

And, imagine this: I actually really like peanut butter and jelly sandwiches!

And this: I had a lifetime of no debt (other than car payments). If I didn't have any cash, I simply didn't spend. Sometimes I made it into a sort of game. What is the cheapest way to eat? Of course, not being a "foodie" helped.

I have been down to my last nickel numerous times. I also made it a habit to not tell anyone. I just told God.[12] He's my Heavenly Father. He never runs short. He never loses track of me. He never forgets me.

What He DOES is… hear my prayers. Every single one.

He does search my heart.

He does nudge me when I need a little nudging.

He does forgive me every single time I confess my sin.

He does restore my joy!

He's a good, good Father.

---

[12] You might remember when I learned that lesson. It was the story of George Mueller.

CHAPTER 28

2019: Financial Journey part 1

Mickey and I recently celebrated reaching a huge financial goal. We became completely debt free!

This is a goal we have worked toward since we first married. We actually had a good start. Both of us had lived our lives nearly debt-free. The two of us took on a hefty mortgage to buy our house. We loved the house and thought we would live in it the rest of our lives.

We then began building a real estate portfolio together. Mickey had done this with his ex for many years, primarily buying houses in foreclosure and then either renting them out or doing some fix-up-clean-up and selling them for a profit.

I was on a learning curve with this, but I love learning new things, so the two of us made a good team. It became a wonderful source of income for us.

Until… the market crashed. We were living north of Orlando, which was one of the worst regions to be hit by the financial crash. Values of the homes we owned at the time dropped about 50%. That was a game-changer.

In addition to our own home, we owned four homes that were occupied by renters (the home I had lived in, the condo Mickey had lived in, plus two homes we had purchased). With the real estate market in freefall, the rental market took a hit too. That meant that the rental income dropped, making it harder for us to pay the mortgages and maintenance on these homes.

Time to trust God… all over again!

A lot of people were simply walking away from their mortgaged homes. Truly, we didn't know if the day would come when we just didn't have the money to pay for our own home, or any of the rental homes we owned.

But as we prayed, we made this solid decision: As long as God provided, we would continue making the monthly payments. If the day ever came when we simply ran out of money, well, we'd cross that bridge when we came to it.

We just really, really wanted to pay back every single dime we owed. In my heart, I always believed that God would come through for us. As long as we followed Him the best we could, He would provide for us. I believed we would indeed pay off every dime.

Somehow we squeaked through. That's another whole story, some of which is written in the book Mickey and I wrote together.[13] In 2016 we moved to The Villages, Florida, where we had family. Two of my sisters and a brother-in-law had moved there a few years ago, and we had been visiting them for holidays and other visits. We loved The Villages, and moving there was a good move for us.

The real estate market had slowly recovered, which meant we could actually sell our own home and then begin selling the rentals we owned. One by one, we sold them. Each time, we paid off more debt (mortgages).

Here's a favorite story! We were putting one of our rental homes on the market and called the realtor we had used previously. We told him we wanted to push the envelope some and start the listing with a fairly high price. Then if we didn't even get offers, we could lower the price. He is the expert, and he really thought our starting price was high. But he agreed to list it as requested.

Within days we had an offer! Not just a "full price" offer, but a full-price-PLUS-another $10,000!

Wow! Did I tell you God is really, really good?

---

[13] *Simply Trusting God*

CHAPTER 29

Financial Journey part 2

By early 2019 we still owned two rental homes north of Orlando. Both homes had older, retired, long-term renters in place. Both qualified as "world's best renters," and we didn't really want to put them out on the street and hope for a quick sale at top price. So we continued renting to them.

And then, suddenly without warning, God seemed to step in to help!

We got a call from the daughter of one of our renters. It seemed that our renter's adult children were noticing some early dementia in our renter and really wanted to move her in to live with them. Their question was: would we allow her to terminate her lease early?

Well, yes! This allowed us to sell the home without having to put her out of the home she had lived in for nine years. We spoke with our renter directly to make sure she was in the loop with all this, and she was.

So we agreed to end the lease as requested.

We also began to strategize on the best way to proceed. In the end, we signed a contract to sell the home "as is" to a wholesaler with a cash offer. Our renter moved out the end of February, leaving the home spotless, and we happily returned her entire security deposit to her.

Because that home had equity, selling it gave us some liquid cash even after paying off the mortgage. Our CPA advised us on how much to hold in reserve for the IRS.

We prayed, strategized, and paid off the remaining bond on our own home (over $20,000). That was a fun day! Definitely some Happy Dancing going on that day! We headed to Panera Bread for a breakfast treat & celebration.

A few months later, we traded in our aging van (2006) and bought a newer (2015) shiny model. We had driven the 2006 van for ten years. God willing, this newer model should last us another ten!

That left us with one rental home remaining. It was by far the home most difficult to sell. It had been my own home before Mickey and I got married.

It still had two mortgages on it, the first mortgage and a second mortgage (HELOC – home equity line of credit) opened to help me pay for it way back then.

When the market crashed, followed by rent prices dropping, we refinanced the first mortgage in an attempt to lower the monthly payments.

Here's the bottom line: We wanted to pay back every dime. So even though refinancing added $5,000 to the principal balance we owed, still, it lowered the monthly payments. And that at least gave us a chance to keep paying. As long as we could, we determined to keep paying. Every month.

God, please help us.

As the real estate market recovered, it finally recovered enough that maybe, just maybe we could sell this home for enough money to pay off those two mortgages. Just barely. Maybe.

Here's another curious thing: That second mortgage? Because it was a HELOC, the bank only required payments of interest for ten years. That's the only reason the rent collected could pay for both mortgages.

After ten years, normally the bank required payment in full, or else we would have to convert the HELOC into a ten-year mortgage to pay back principal and interest. We had been through this with another home.

Problem: If we had to start paying off the principal, the rent wouldn't be enough to cover these payments. Not to mention paying the HOA and occasional maintenance.

But this bank *never asked* for payment. The ten-year mark came and went. We kept paying only interest, sometimes throwing in a bit more if we were able.

We were concerned that IF the bank did contact us, asking for payment of the principal ($42,000), we might have to default. We really, truly did not have enough money coming in to pay an extra mortgage.

So from 2005 (when I first bought the home) until 2019 (way past ten years), we only paid interest on the second mortgage.

In 2019, we asked the renters in the home if they had any interest in buying the home. And… they said YES!

Selling a home to the renter in place is the best way to sell. We had done that before, and it's a win/win. The renter knows the home well, knows the neighbors, knows how all appliances work, etc. There are no surprises to the renter/buyer.

For us, it meant that we continued receiving rent money right up to the day of closing. The renter/buyer doesn't even have to pay for an inspection if they don't want to. And another advantage to us was, we had no realtor commission to pay (usually several thousand dollars).

So in October 2019, we sold this last rental home, closing with enough to pay off those two mortgages in full! There was no real money left over for us. We did, however, celebrate with a dinner out! We headed to one of our favorite restaurants: Olive Garden! Planned to arrive before 4:00 for the early bird pricing! So perfect!

And with that closing, we were finally completely, 100% debt-free! Mickey and I went through several days – maybe weeks – of spontaneous Happy Dances!

Actually, I think it was months!

> *God's fingerprints are all over this! Holding us steady through many years of making payments with no sure way of paying them off. I think God honored that.*

I did know this: It made us very happy. Joyful! And giving God all the glory!

CHAPTER 30

1968 – 2019 (Serving God)

From the beginning, I have loved serving the amazing God I was learning so much about. At my very first church (then known as Brighton Community Church), I helped in the preschool class.

Two years later, when I moved onto campus to begin college, there was only one church I could get to within walking distance, so that's where I went. Right on campus. I soon found a place to serve: high school teens. I loved teaching the high school Sunday School class.

After getting married and moving to Kansas City, we were asked to be part of an undercover ministry. The idea was that every new person who visited our church would be assigned to a leadership couple for follow-up, including phone calls and invitations to our home. I enjoyed that. The leadership couples met about once a month to share ideas, encourage each other, and sometimes to swap assignments if needed.

Then was Pennsylvania, where I was primarily known as the Pastor's Wife, but also served in children's ministry as well as women's ministry. I taught children's classes as well as women's groups.

Maryland, was next, and I served as the Director of Women's Ministries. I also was part of a ladies' trio, singing worship songs in three-part harmony. I loved that.

From there, we moved to Warren, Pennsylvania, where we stayed for many years. I served on the Teen Council, taught children's Sunday School classes, Vacation Bible School classes, and maybe my favorite: Bible Quiz Coach. At first I helped in the children's Bible Quizzing program because that's where my own children were. But when my oldest moved into 7th grade and wanted to participate in Teen Bible Quizzing, there was no coach. I was somewhat reluctantly drafted into coaching a team.

This was a fairly intense program and required significant time for me to prepare and lead. It was fun though, and meaningful to teens. I especially loved finding ways to let my own love for Jesus show up.

After the separation, I resigned from all my church positions. It made sense, partly because I was such a mess and needed time to heal. For the first time in my adult life, I did not volunteer to serve in church. I couldn't.

When divorce was finally, mercifully final, I moved to Rochester, where instead of serving, I signed up to receive help through their Stephens Ministry – a compassionate one-on-one program to walk individual people through a season of crisis. Parenting my daughter as a single mom threw me into some crisis moments.

I needed help. Without question. Many days, the one-on-one weekly meeting was a lifeline for me. I also signed up to go through the church's Divorce Recovery program, another healing program for me.

After moving to central Florida, I soon volunteered as a small group facilitator in my church's Divorce Recovery program. This was a ministry that served hurting people and I was thankful that my own experience and healing process could help others. Every time I led a new group through a 13-week class, it was review time for me.

Now in my retirement years, it saddens me that I can no longer volunteer in the usual ways. My physical health limitations have closed doors. I try to be a friendly face and greeting in our Sunday School class and at the church service. One reason we love our class is because there are usually several homeless people who come. There is a food table that volunteers fill with various breakfast food and that is a welcome treat for the homeless and everyone else.

Every Sunday, I look for the homeless so I can at least greet them. One week as I was talking to two of the women, the conversation quickly turned to being ready for death (someone we all knew had just died). I asked each of them if they were ready for death; one said yes, the other said no. I reviewed the gospel for her, and as time ran out (it was time for the class to begin), I reminded her there would be an opportunity to respond at the end of the church service. And then I prayed!

Somehow I am drawn to the homeless. It always seems that these are "my" people. Maybe because I knew where I came from. Remember?

During this stage of my life, it may be that my main contribution to building the kingdom is to be faithful in prayer. I do not view that meaningful time as "less than" other more active, more visible service.

And when our pastor closes each service, he comes down from the stage to stand at the front of the church to invite people to come forward in response to the sermon. After he speaks with them briefly, he motions to someone (sometimes Mickey for men, or me for women); we are trained to take the person to a private room where we ask what the need is. We pray with the person, and write down the contact information for follow-up by the church. Mickey and I are glad to serve in this way.

CHAPTER 31

Spiritual Training for the Kids

I want to include a memory about when I was raising my young children. I homeschooled the three kids to about 5th grade, and made it a practice to begin each day with Bible reading and prayer.

Basically, I wanted to introduce them to the concept of daily Bible reading and prayer. I did this each morning before we began regular school work. I did it different ways through the years.

One way the kids seemed to like was to take my well worn Bible and randomly open to any page and then see what has been underlined there. I am a big underliner, and I really like reading through the entire Bible, cover to cover. Over and over. There are very few pages with no underlining at all. So that sort of worked. One of the kids would randomly open the Bible and point to an underlined verse. I would read aloud the underlined verse, and talk about it. I explained why it is underlined, and what it means to me.

Later, as the kids were older, I sometimes incorporated the Bible Quizzing curriculum and used whatever book of the Bible that was being studied that year. I would read a section from that book. We would read straight through the book, beginning each day where we left off the day before. And then start over again. This helped the kids get familiar with one book at a time, and then we would talk about what it meant.

I have many sweet memories of this morning practice. I hope – and still pray – that those times are still bearing fruit.

CHAPTER 32

Spiritual Connection

After my initial separation and ultimately divorce, I was pretty badly bruised and bleeding (emotionally). But spiritually? No. Not really.

I have written about the days and weeks and months of sitting on the floor with my Bible open, drinking in the Words of truth I so badly needed. In spite of the years of emotional damage, I really never doubted God's goodness. I knew I could lean on Him, and I did.

I remember learning through the Divorce Recovery program that you need a year of recovery for every five years of marriage, so at the age of 45 (when separation occurred), I began to look forward to turning 50. Maybe by then I would feel more balanced. Like I could walk on my own two feet. No more limping through each day.

And truly, that's kind of how it went. I rejoiced when I turned 50! I was ready to face whatever the future might hold. At the age of 50, I did indeed feel a sense of balance return.

During those five years, I worked hard on recovery. I went to professional counselors. I read books. I went to group therapy to help me process. One was a 12-step program for codependent addicts to recover. Every week, around the circle, "Hi, my name is Cindy and I am a codependent."

Another was my church's Divorce Recovery program. And once I began facilitating groups in Divorce Recovery, it was sort of like a continuation of my own recovery.

Later, when I first met Mickey, we spent a lot of our early conversations telling each other about our histories. Our messy, complicated histories.

Mickey was curious about one thing in particular. He asked me why I didn't just walk away from God? It didn't make sense to him. Obviously, serving God didn't work, right?

On the surface, my story may have looked like a failure on God's part. But truly, nothing could have been further from the truth! Not even close. The failure of my marriages was absolutely a failure on the part of the two people involved. And maybe it's fair to say that it was also a partial victory for Satan – always the enemy of our souls.

Couldn't God have fixed it? Yes, of course He could have. So, why didn't that happen?

The short answer is: we humans make choices.

God never wanted to make puppets. He made us with the ability to make our own decisions.

We can make wonderful, unselfish choices, generally resulting in better outcomes.

Or we are free to make selfish, mean, awful choices, generally resulting in harm for self and/or others.

Making marriage work well takes two people. Making a marriage disaster can be done by just one person.

That was one of the hard realities I had to learn from my counselors and books I read. It sort of goes along with this classic truth:

You can only change one person: you. You cannot change another person.

That was one of the basic boundary issues I had to learn.

Therefore, if my marriage (or any relationship) becomes unsatisfactory, I need to look at myself first. What did I do to contribute to this problem? I can make changes in the way I conduct myself. I might wish the other person would change, but I cannot force that.

What I can do is change my own behavior. Shake things up a bit. The changes will probably be apparent to the other person, and that might incentivize them to make some changes that are healthier.

If my changes don't yield anything different at all from the other person, then I have learned something valuable. At that point, I can decide if I can live with it, or I can remove myself.

My marriage to George failed because both of us were contributing to the downward spiral. Yes, I really had contributed to this failure! So, yes, I could change.

What happened then was this: As I slowly became healthier, insisting (mostly not with words, but with action) that I would be "treated well, or not at all," the more my dysfunctional marriage didn't work.

The fact that he initiated the hasty ending and then remarried so quickly reinforced my own suspicions that divorce was his goal from the start. Being an ordained minister in a conservative denomination, however, meant that he could never admit that.

Notice how none of that has anything to do with God. God hates divorce! So do I. Especially due to the profound impact it has on children, even adult children.

In the end, I had to ask each of my children to please forgive me, and then I had to ask my God to forgive me too.

Probably hardest of all was for me to accept God's forgiveness.

All of it takes time.

From those days until now, I live life bearing scars and wounds from my many years of brokenness. Even as God showed His grace and forgiveness… Even though He has opened up a whole new life with Mickey, still… the scars remain.

I'm okay with that. I have made my peace with God. Even Jesus bears scars. Maybe scars are God's way of reminding us… He alone brings healing.

May God always be praised!

CHAPTER 33

It's All About the Gospel

Throughout the years and decades of this spiritual journey, I have always had a heart for sharing the gospel with anyone who doesn't yet know the goodness of God. With each passing year, God has shown Himself to be better than I could ever imagine.

For real!

It always seemed to me that if someone only knew how good God was, it's sort of a no-brainer to give up everything if it means you end up with Him. (That includes material "stuff" as well as reputation.) That's a really great deal!

My early attempts to tell others about my great God were predictably clumsy and not very clear. Still, I took advantage of any and all classes on personal evangelism. I read books and articles about how to share the good news with others. With the advent of the internet, more help was available, and I took it all in. I still do.

Mickey tells me often that it was only after meeting me that he became interested in learning more about Jesus. That used to shock me. But it makes sense to me in a very sad way. Mickey met me when he was in his mid-forties. Raised Jewish, he must have met Christians throughout his life. Was there no one who piqued his interest?

Yes, he says, there was one. A guy from high school. He told Mickey that classic C.S. Lewis argument. He asked Mickey: who do you think Jesus was? Mickey said what he'd been trained to say: Jesus was a good teacher, a good rabbi, a good prophet. But C.S. Lewis argued that you cannot say Jesus was merely a good teacher.

> "I am trying here to prevent anyone saying the really foolish thing that people often say about Him: I'm ready to accept Jesus as a great moral teacher, but I don't accept his claim to be God. That is the one thing we must not say. A man who was merely a man and said the sort of things Jesus said would not be a great moral teacher. He would either be a lunatic—on the level with the man who says he is a poached egg—or else he would be the Devil of Hell. You must make your choice. Either this man was, and is, the Son of God, or else a madman or something worse. You can shut him up for a fool, you can spit at him and kill him as a demon or you can fall at his feet and call him Lord and God, but let us not come

with any patronising nonsense about his being a
great human teacher. He has not left that open to
us. He did not intend to. . . . Now it seems to me
obvious that He was neither a lunatic nor a fiend:
and consequently, however strange or terrifying
or unlikely it may seem, I have to accept the view
that He was and is God" (*Mere Christianity, p.*
55-56).

Liar, Lunatic, or Lord? Jesus has to be one or the other.

Mickey says there is one thing that changed everything for him: seeing me live my life of faith with integrity. My behavior and actions were consistent with my words. Everyone else he had met who said they were Christian lived life pretty much the same as he did. Lying was normal. Mickey lied often, but so did everyone, including people who said they were "Christians." Deception? Sure! Manipulation? Yep! So why should he be interested in following Jesus?

I am thrilled that Mickey could see Jesus in me! Of course back then, I didn't dream that Mickey would someday become my husband! When it all fell into place for him, I watched him with tears flowing. He finally understood the impact of what Jesus had gone through... for him. He bowed his head and prayed, asking God to forgive him.

It's always a thrill to see someone respond to the greatest news of all time. God has used me a few times to tell others the gospel. I pray for more opportunities.

From the beginning of time, God created the earth and planted it into the universe He had made, and then He created all the plants and animals. His crowning touch was after the earth itself was perfect, He then created Adam and Eve and placed them into a beautiful garden setting. They were perfect; it was all perfect.

The plan was to enjoy the earth, explore it, and take care of it. All while walking and talking with God Himself every day.

Everything was so wonderful. Just the way it was supposed to be. It was good. It was very good.

And yet, God did give them free will. The one command God gave them they disobeyed. Adam and Eve did the one thing God said no to. With that one momentous act of disobedience, sin entered the human race. Every single one of us from Adam on has done the same. We are all guilty. We are all sinners.

But God, in His goodness, did not leave us without a remedy. His love for us was so great that He put a cosmic plan in place to rescue us.

Slowly, He began to reveal His plan. That plan is detailed in the pages of the Bible. The Old Testament reveals God's nature and character as He begins to show people that no matter how much they tried, they could never really be good. The laws God gave were largely to prove that point.

We were going to need a rescue plan.

And then, at just the right time, Jesus left the glories of heaven to become a crying, messy, newborn infant. God Himself put on flesh and became a human. He was the perfect man, and He willingly became the sacrifice we needed to pay for our sins. He didn't need it; we did.

It was a grand swap! I gave up my mountain pile of sins in exchange for His forgiveness, His goodness, His character.

On the very day I said "yes" to Him, my new life was like a garden to Him. He planted seeds deep in my soul; they sprouted and slowly grew into God's character. My life-garden began to blossom and then grow into the fruit He was growing in me: love, joy, peace, patience, kindness, goodness, faithfulness, gentleness, and self-control (Galatians 5:22-23). It was amazing!

If you have never tasted the deliciousness of God's pure grace, maybe it's time. Right now. Why not?

Will tomorrow be better? What if you don't have a "tomorrow" at all? What if you knew today was your last day on earth?

You have everything to gain and really… nothing to lose. At least nothing that's worth much.

So today – right now – make this your moment. Let's go. Let's do this!

God, right now, I bow in Your presence. I realize that I have been living my whole life the way I wanted it, never really considering what others might want. Or what YOU want.

I believe You. Jesus, You are the very Son of God. I believe that You died on that cross for me! To pay the price for my own sins. Please forgive me! I really want to live the rest of my life serving You. I sort of can't wait to begin! Thank you, Jesus. Thank you for being my Savior.

In Jesus' name, Amen.

CHAPTER 34

Epilogue

I am now happily owning birthday #70. God has been good to me, allowing me to check off another decade. Each day, each year, each decade brings me that much closer to the day I will finally see Him face to face. That will be the best day of my life! How could it not be?

As I reflect on the years, a few things remain strong in my life. One is the deep, profound sense of grief I still carry over the impact my divorce had on my three children. I have read that it really never goes away. Even with adult children, it changes them and the way they view the world. There is just no getting around that.

That thought alone can really drive me into dark sadness. Even though I have tried very hard to identify how I contributed to divorce, even though I have said "I'm sorry" to each of my children countless times, still… I can't not know that it impacts them negatively still.

I am sorry. Still, today. I am profoundly sorry.

As the years and decades roll on, I continue facing ongoing health problems. The fatigue continues growing. And these days, I have a sense that even my memory and cognitive functions are slowing down. But I'm pretty comfortable facing the future solidly following Jesus. With Mickey by my side.

Being in this marriage, after two disaster marriages, is still amazing to me. God's grace just splashed all over me with Mickey. I did not earn this. I did not deserve this. This marriage is a pure straight out gift to me from God Himself.

Mickey and I are partners in every sense. We laugh together. We seriously try to outdo each other in serving each other. When needed, we gently point out issues that arise and work together to regain balance.

And joy.

Oh yes… definitely joy!

Worshiping our God together? That's like nothing else in life.

Marriage really doesn't work very well if only one partner is committed to Jesus and to the marriage. That dynamic almost guarantees failure, or at best, a tolerable life.

As I grow older, I begin looking forward to my real homecoming. I know God has been preparing a place for me, and sometimes... I almost can't wait.

But He hasn't yet called me home, so I know He still has plans for me here. It is my highest goal to live each day serving Him. Every single day.

I have learned some things. God doesn't change. He is the same God every day, every minute. He loves to invite me right into His presence where He is always ready to bless me, challenge me, rebuke me, or sometimes gently correct me. I am thankful for it all.

Anything that comes to me from God is welcome in my life. During the stormy seasons, He is especially trustworthy. Oftentimes, that's when I am especially drawn to Him. I may come before Him more than just the usual morning time. And each time I do, He is ready to welcome me into His presence. I don't think I'll ever get over that. Seriously.

I have found Him to be true. As long as I stay close to Him, I really can't go too wrong.

He is faithful!

One of my new favorite songs played on my local Christian radio station. "Well Done" by the Afters.

What will it be like when my pain is gone
And all the worries of this world just fade away?
What will it be like when You call my name
And that moment when I see You face to face?
I'm waiting my whole life to hear You say...

Well done, well done!
My good and faithful one
Welcome to the place where you belong.
Well done, well done!
My beloved child
Waiting my whole life for that day
Until then I'll live to hear You say...

Well done, well done!
My good and faithful one
Welcome to the place where you belong
Well done, well done!
My beloved child
You have run the race and now you're home
Welcome to the place where you belong
Well done!

PHOTOS

That's me on the right, with my
scowling face!

maybe 7?

maybe 10?
Before glasses. No budding beauty queen here!

High school

no more glasses

2006

Our wedding day

The family home where I grew up. Still owned by one of my brothers

2019

ABOUT THE AUTHOR

Cindy Mallin is first of all a joyful follower of Christ! After raising three children (now all grown), and homeschooling them during their early years, she is now a grandmother of seven. She is amazed to be in an incredibly happy marriage to Mickey, a wonderful Jewish man who gave his heart to Jesus in 2006 and never looked back. Follow her on Twitter: @cindymallin.